From Wiltshire to Wales

*The story of the Palmer family of Coombe Bissett
and Cardiff from the fourteenth century
to the twentieth century*

Ray Palmer

From Wiltshire to Wales
The story of the Palmer family
of Coombe Bissett and Cardiff
from the fourteenth century to
the twentieth century
Ray Palmer

Design ©131 Design Ltd
www.131design.org
Text & images ©Ray Palmer

ISBN 978-1-909660-63-2

A CIP catalogue record for this book
is available from the British Library

Published 2016 by Tricorn Books
131 High Street, Old Portsmouth
PO1 2HW

www.tricornbooks.co.uk

Printed and bound in UK

From Wiltshire
to Wales

To Debbie & Paul.

It's all about family!
Enjoy "the journey"...

Dad / Ray

Contents

Chap has to be careful or else he would soon go under as we are now, but thank God we have our health and strength and each other, and we are bound closer together by our misfortune.

Alfred Palmer, diary entry, 1913

Preface

This is the story of an ordinary family. It's a large family, but an ordinary one nonetheless. In the pages that follow you won't read of ancestors who sailed on the *Mayflower*, or who witnessed Anne Boleyn's execution, or who rode in the Charge of the Light Brigade, or who flew Spitfires. At least, if any of them did I haven't found out ... yet!

This is, however, a story of a family steeped in the principle of hard work, who through at least six centuries and many generations have strived to give their children a reasonable start in life and a good Christian home. It is a story of extremes, of a successful settled and respected family who suddenly and through no fault of their own fall upon hard times, and then some generations later and through their own efforts turn their fortunes around again. Like most families, they had their share of tragedies, some of which we cannot begin to imagine today; but there are also indications of much happiness and very strong family bonds. And you'll spot a few rogues along the way.

I have tried to give a flavour of their lives over many generations, though perhaps inevitably the stories about more recent ones are rather more detailed than the accounts of earlier ancestors. The story is predominantly about the direct line down to me from my ancestors. Occasionally I have added some detail about relatives who are not on that direct line where there is something of special interest to tell. I should also make it clear that, save for one passage, I have followed the paternal line back from me: this has taken several years' work, and to extend it into the maternal line would just not be feasible – for me at least!

Much of the information I have used has come from publicly available official records, though I have also tapped into the memories and collections of more recent generations. They have collected and retained papers, photographs, correspondence, and of course memories and stories handed down, because there is a fascination about one's heritage, and for some people a desire to discover and preserve what made them what they are today.

This book is an attempt to bring this wealth of material together for the benefit of the many people who still bear one of the surnames that has derived from, or merged with, the Palmer line, and for those too young to understand but who one day might experience the same curiosity.

Dylan Thomas started his masterpiece *Under Milk Wood* with the words 'To begin at the beginning'. Well that's an excellent first line when you're making up a story. But when you're trying to write a family history you know very well that the first piece of the story you're writing about is not really the beginning. You know that ancestors lived and things happened for generations before the first one you're writing about, but you just can't trace enough information to write confidently about those times.

So it is with this book. As I take you forward through the centuries, you'll see that a few intelligent guesses are mixed with probabilities, probabilities are supported by historical facts, and historical facts are borne out by first-hand accounts. Bear with me, then, as I move through the early days where – even though I have many historical facts and have accessed some key documents – I have now and again made some informed assumptions. And if you are occasionally left asking 'but what happened to Tom ... or Dick ... or Harry?', then rest assured that I will have asked that question many times myself, and have simply been unable to find an answer.

I've included a relevant section of the family tree at the start of most chapters; to have included the full family tree would have made this book considerably larger, so I have broken the tree down into sections that are relevant to the chapters in the hope that this will help the reader to follow the key characters in the story. To make it simpler to follow I have in some instances also omitted family members from the tree who are not mentioned in the chapter.

I have used a large number of sources, and I acknowledge these at the end of this book. But it is right that I should acknowledge here the many members of my family, some of whom I had neither met nor heard of before I started this research, for their assistance and contributions. Those I did not know previously I have traced through a variety of methods, and they have responded to my approaches with enthusiasm.

Part One: Roots

The Early Centuries

1

What's in a name?

*L*et's start with a word about the Palmer name. In 2014, there were estimated to be over 300,000 people in the world bearing the surname Palmer, about 48,000 of them in England, and 2,700 in Wales.

This ancient Anglo-French surname, recorded variously as Palmer, Palmar, Parmer and Paumier, and the dialectals (regional variations) Pymar, Pymer, and Pimer, is a medieval descriptive nickname. It is one of the many early European surnames that gradually evolved from the habitual use of personal descriptions or characteristics. The name comes from the pre-tenth-century Old French 'palmer' or 'paumier', and derives from assumed or actual pilgrimages or crusades to the Holy Land. The pilgrims generally brought back a palm branch as proof that they had actually made the journey: as a quotation from a medieval writer reads,

> *The faded palm-branch in his hand, showed the pilgrim from the Holy Land.*

In its various spellings this was one of the earliest of all surnames. Early recorded examples of the surname include Wiger le Palmer of Lincolnshire in 1191, and Richard le Paumere of Middlesex in 1198. John le Paumer, Walter le Paumer and William le Paumer are all referred to in records of criminal proceedings in Wiltshire in 1268. John Palmer, aged 18 years, who embarked from London on the ship *Primrose* bound for Virginia in July 1635, was one of the earliest recorded settlers in America.

Perhaps more relevant to my story is the Tax List for 1332 for the village of Coombe Bissett in Wiltshire, which is the location for much of my story, and where thirty people – mostly men – had to pay tax. Their names might read rather like a modern telephone directory from mainland Europe, or more likely from a work by Chaucer: Artoys, Atte Mulle, Govayre, Henryes, le Bakere, le Couke, and so on. A Ricardus le Palmere was serving on the manorial court of Coombe Bissett in May 1307. But the name that jumped out of the list for me was Roger le Palmere, a name clearly of Anglo-French origin and, although I cannot establish a link, quite possibly one of my earliest recorded ancestors. Roger undoubtedly complained to all who might listen about his 1332 tax assessment, which required him to pay sixteen and a half pence (in pre-decimalisation UK money).

Next, I must introduce you to the Barber family. You will read more about them later, because on a number of occasions Palmer men married Barber women. That happened during the early 1700s, but I'm going back now to the late Middle Ages, and the middle of the fourteenth century, soon after the Hundred Years' War began, when Edward III with the Black Prince and their outnumbered army defeated the French at Crécy. Around this time, there was a family called Waylot living in the village of Durrington, north of Salisbury and close to Stonehenge. The Waylots were bondsmen of Winchester College, to which they were bound in a number of ways to provide services in return for their tenure of land owned by the College, and would remain so for the next two centuries.

But there was a problem: there were rather too many people called Waylot living in one small village. So people would change their surname to reflect their occupation. Welsh readers might recognise a similar concept which led to people being known as 'Jones the Milk' or 'Thomas the Bread', in order to distinguish them from many other Joneses or Thomases. So Mr Waylot the carter (who made carts) became Waylot alias Carter, and Mr Waylot who cut the villagers' hair became Waylot alias Barber. The marriage of a woman called Barber into the Palmer family means that I am in part descended from a village barber who lived near Stonehenge at around the time of the Black Death in the mid-fourteenth century, and whose family moved to Coombe Bissett in the fifteenth century.

Other names emerge from time to time during this story. Coombe Bissett was a small village, and the residents hardly ever moved away before the end of the nineteenth century. So mingling with the Palmers in rural Wiltshire you will see names like Lawes, Harwood, Lush, Meaden and Macklin, whose families spent several centuries in Coombe Bissett or in villages close by. This actually makes research problematic, firstly because as time passed and families grew there were large numbers of them with the same name in the same place, and secondly because – as the saying goes – they lived in each other's pockets, a situation which sometimes reached extremes as the Coombe Bissett 'Bastardy Examination Index' confirms!

2

What's in a place?

At this point it might help the reader to know a little about Coombe Bissett, because along with the neighbouring villages of Homington and Stratford Tony it was the centre of the Palmer family history for several centuries. Coombe Bissett is a small village in the valley of the River Ebble, about four miles south-west of Salisbury, in Wiltshire. The name of the village has had many spelling variations over the centuries, ranging from the simple Come (1086) to the rather grand Coumbe Byset Super Ebelesburne (1288). The name derives from *cumb*, an ancient word for a valley. Today it's affectionately (if perhaps unkindly) referred to by some locals as 'Crumbly Biscuit'. Homington, which has also had several name variations, means *Humma's Farm.*

At the time of the Domesday survey, Coombe Bissett was a royal manor. There was enough land to keep twenty ploughs busy, namely sixty acres of meadow and pasture and ten acres of small wood. In the medieval period the manorial flocks of Coombe Bissett totalled between 100 and 500 sheep. In Homington there were six acres of pasture and three acres of meadow.

At that time the church of Coombe Bissett was controlled by Leofric the priest, and the one at Homington by Osbern the priest. In the thirteenth century the de Plessettis (or Plessys) controlled the village. The historian Richard Colt Hoare notes that in 1275:

> *Hugh de Plessy and John de Wolytton, or Wotton, held one knight's fee of the King in chief, in Cumbe, by reason of their wives; and they claimed to have gallows and the assize of bread and ale.*

By 1303 the heir to the estate had changed his name from Wotton to Biset.

The following generation saw Hugh de Plessetis and John Byset as heirs to the estate. Both were under age and wards of the King. During the reign of King Edward III the manor was still divided into portions. By 1394 the Knight Walter de Romeseye held the manor of Combe in Wiltshire.

Coombe Bissett had 159 tax payers in 1377 and Homington had 116. The population of the parish of Coombe Bissett rose steadily to 271 in 1801 and to 415 in 1851, although thereafter the figure drops, largely due to migration to larger towns in the area. Population figures for Homington, though smaller, followed a similar trend. The majority of buildings in the parish were made of Flemish bond brick; roofs were either thatched with wheat straw or tiled. By the time that formal censuses were taken in the nineteenth century, most of the population of Coombe Bissett were farm labourers, although there were also servants, an ostler, carpenter, carters, coal and wood merchants, masons, dressmakers, grooms, farm bailiffs, and dressmakers. A national school was built in 1845. Around that time the main crops of both parishes were wheat, barley and turnips, while near Coombe Bissett's old pack-horse bridge were watercress beds which were seasonally regenerated by sprinkling plants on the surface of the water with a pronged fork, to be harvested at a later date.

There is evidence of a smithy in Coombe Bissett in 1671, when his premises included a brewhouse, milkhouse, buttery and blacksmith's shop, though by 1801 the smithy was situated opposite the church. The church of St. Michael and All Angels is built of stone and flint, its earliest features dating from the twelfth century (picture 1).

In the nineteenth century there was a beer house run from a cottage in the village by Mary Meaden, a surname that will appear later in this story; no doubt it was a popular haunt for the Palmer family, although perhaps the centre of village life was the inn known as the Fox and Goose: for sure it is a place that crops up from time to time in the Palmer history. The inn was on the Turnpike Road, where the toll collector resided at the Toll House.

Finally, it's worth mentioning that for a while there was a habit of naming houses after the names of families. The reader will recall some of the surnames mentioned thus far, and should note that in the 1851 census there were three properties named Meadens, one named Barbers, and two named Palmers. The names are probably historic, deriving from former holders of the land. Houses (and lands which went with them) in Coombe Bissett frequently had names attached to them that sometimes endured for centuries. For instance one of the tenancies in the manor of Winchester College was called Palmers, doubtless taking its name from a tenant called John Palmer who died towards the end of the fifteenth century; over 200 years and six generations later, it was still called Palmers.

A map at Appendix B shows the locations of the main villages and towns that feature in the Wiltshire part of the story.

Violence and charity

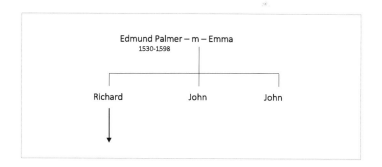

I will begin with Edmund Palmer. He was my great-great-great-great-great-great-great-great-great-great-great-grandfather (to save the reader counting, that's eleven 'greats'), and the earliest of my identifiable ancestors. He was born around 1530, when King Henry VIII was trying to rid himself firstly of his wife Catherine of Aragon, and secondly of the Roman Catholic Church in England.

Edmund and his wife Emma had three sons called Richard, John and ... John (a curious habit, to which I shall return). Like most of those who will follow, and no doubt those before him, Edmund and his family lived in Coombe Bissett. He was a husbandman, a tenant farmer who worked the land growing wheat and barley, rearing and looking after sheep and cattle, and selling the produce in local markets.

These were not easy times, and the first patent roll of the reign of Elizabeth I records what must have been a frightening incident involving Edmund. On a day in November 1556 he was driving a cart loaded with a huge stock of valuable soft goods, including coverlets, cushions, and woollen cloth. They included a coverlet described as *'a coveringe of silke with ymages'* worth £6. 13s 4d; two other coverlets worth £5. 6s 8d; *'a large coverlet with flowers and conys'* (rabbits) worth £2. 6s 8d, two other coverlets with *'conies'* worth £4, another coverlet called *'a vennys carpet'*, and eighteen *'cowshins'* (cushions) worth £4. Quite why Edmund, a farmer, was conveying such goods is a mystery: they were not his usual stock in trade, and it is unlikely that he was involved with the production or sale of such fine goods. More likely is that he was making a little extra money by delivering them for somebody else. He was accompanied by Thomas Redde, a yeoman, also from Coombe Bissett. A yeoman was a farmer who might have owned some land, a little above a husbandman in terms of class, so perhaps Edmund was merely driving Redde's cart.

As they steered the cart across Broad Chalke Down they were attacked by four men, namely William Fere, Nicholas Hunt, William Berter and John Gefferies, all from across the county border in Dorset. The robbery was ferocious: the highwaymen attacked Edmund and Thomas with violence and arms, and struck, wounded and maltreated them so that they despaired of their lives. The attackers were indicted for robbery, although it seems that one – William Fere – received a royal pardon three years later.

Edmund obviously recovered from his injuries, and survived for over forty years until he died in 1598. He had executed his Will shortly before he died while he was

> *… sick in bodie but whole in mind and remembraunce thankes be to god …*

He bequeathed twelve pence to the Parish Church, and

> *…to the poore of the parisshe one Bushell of Barly …*

He left a number of sheep to his three sons, Richard, John and …. John (picture 2).

Edmund's wife Emma also executed her Will in 1598. She too admitted to being

> *... sicke in body but of perfect minde and memory ...,*

although she survived her husband by five or six years. Emma's Will confirmed the existence of two sons called John the elder and John the younger. She also left a bushel of barley to the poor of the parish, and

> *...fower sheep and a steer bullock ...*

to her grandson called – yes – John, with the request to her executors that the steer bullock was to be mated with the cow bullock before the grandson claimed it. She left John the elder

> *... an aker wheat and an aker barly, not best nor worste but such as my overseers shall thinke good, and more to him 5 sheep ...*

Her son Richard inherited

> *... a great brasse potte ... and to every of his children a sheep ...*

The inventory of Emma's assets shows that in total she owned sixteen sheep and four lambs (picture 3).

There might have been more to the two Johns than meets the eye, and it's likely that the duplication of names reveals rather more than a lack of imagination. Property known as copyhold was held by the custom of the manor, although by the end of the Middle Ages it was much the same as freehold, except that copyhold tenants had to pay a notional rent to the manor, and a fine when they sold the property. Three named persons were nominated: the first-named was the holder tenant and held the property for the duration of their life. The other two effectively formed a queue, so that when the first-named died, the second-named inherited the property and nominated a new third person for the end of the new queue. These were recorded in the court rolls as the 'copyhold' for this type of tenant. So the

Palmers held their land as copyhold tenants of the manor, on leases for a term of three named lives.

But there was a known subterfuge by which a devious tenant would give an identical name to more than one of his children, thereby providing a 'spare' offspring to keep the lease going if one died. Evidence of the ploy came in 1664 at neighbouring Stratford Tony, where the manorial court had to give an assurance that none of the copyholders had christened two children with the same name in order to cheat the lord of the manor. The manorial court was the lowest court of law in England, and governed those areas over which the lord of the manor had jurisdiction. It dealt with copyhold land transfers, managing the open fields, settling disputes between individuals, and manorial offences. It also administered *frankpledge*, at which all men over the age of twelve were bound to appear and make their 'pledge' to keep the king's peace. The court would meet roughly every three weeks throughout the year.

Inheritance and debt

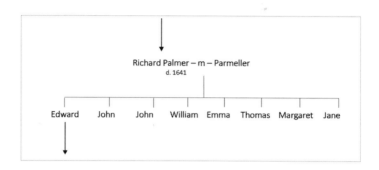

*E*dmund's son Richard was my great-great-great-great-great-great-great-great-great-great-grandfather.

He married a woman called Parmeller, who produced a number of children, namely Edward, William, Emma - who would in due course marry Matthew Turner of Tisbury - Thomas, Margaret, and Jane. And inevitably there were two called John. Richard and one of his brothers John appear on the jury lists for the manorial court lists, respectively from 1601 to 1638 and 1605 to 1629.

Richard died in August 1641 and was buried in Coombe Bissett. His widow Parneller was granted administration, giving a bond to the Dean of Salisbury promising to administer Richard's estate correctly and to produce an inventory of Richard's goods before 1 October on pain of forfeiting £100 to the Dean. She left it a little late, but the inventory was indeed produced in the Dean's court with just one day to spare. The bond for £100 was undertaken jointly by Parmeller and her son Edward, who was described in the document as a husbandman of Stratford Tony.

The inventory of Richard's assets was made on the day of his burial by five *'praysers'* (appraisers). The total value, including corn in the field, bacon, and forty sheep, was £45. 17s 10d. On the back of the inventory is a list of *'deates oing'* (debts owing), totalling £60. 17s 4d. It is unclear whether these were debts owed *by* Richard or debts owed *to* him, but of the nine people named, four are Palmers: John Palmer, William Palmer, Edward Palmer and Thomas Palmer, while others named are Renall Batten and William Lipps and his daughter. William Lipps had married Richard's daughter Margaret in 1614, while Rennall Batten, from Ringwood in Hampshire, had married Richard's daughter Jane Palmer in 1632. So the list includes four sons and at least two sons-in-law of Richard, and it is possible that the list represents the balances of legacies promised by Richard during his lifetime.

Away from home

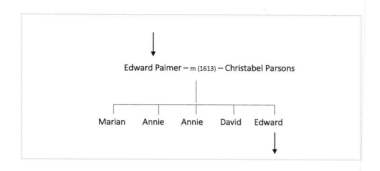

Richard's son Edward Palmer was probably his eldest son, and was my great-great-great-great-great-great-great-great-great-grandfather.

Notwithstanding that the administration bond entered into by his mother referred to Stratford Tony, it seems certain that Edward was essentially a Coombe Bissett man. In 1613 he married a woman called Christabel Parsons in Stratford Tony, where they lived until his father died in 1641. Around that time he returned to Coombe Bissett, possibly to be close to his mother, but more likely to take over his father's tenancy of the land there. He was certainly back in Coombe Bissett in 1644 when his name appeared in the records of the manorial court jury.

Edward and Christabel had at least five children, namely Marian, Annie, another Annie, and David. They had another son whose name was either Edward or Edmund, though I cannot be sure which, who was born in 1628.

These would have been difficult and perhaps fearful times for the simple folk of Coombe Bissett: they might not have understood the intricacies of the growing constitutional differences between King Charles I and Parliament in the 1620s, but they were perhaps only too aware that ordinary hard-working people had to contribute taxes to fund yet another war against the French.

Plots and conspiracies

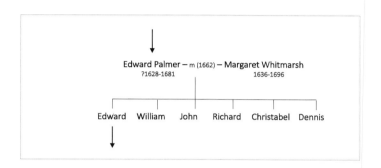

Edward or Edmund was my great-great-great-great-great-great-great-great-grandfather, and for simplicity I will call him Edward. He was born in Coombe Bissett just at the time that a certain Oliver Cromwell made his first appearance in the English parliament.

I don't know much about Edward, who is described as a yeoman. The meaning of 'yeoman' changed over time, and around this time it indicated a member of a class, perhaps a farmer who held and farmed their own land, which might be freehold, leasehold or (as most likely in the Palmer's case) copyhold.

Edward's name appears as a signatory to the Coombe Bissett Protestation Return of 1641-42. The returns recorded statements read to all parishioners, and all men over the age of 18 were required to sign an oath which pledged loyalty to the King, and their opposition to 'Plotts and Conspiracies'. The return was also signed by men of a family called Whitmarsh, to whom I shall return shortly.

Between 1648 and 1667 Edward was recorded as a juryman in the local manorial court, as was his father Edward Palmer senior. In addition to routine three-weekly sessions there were special twice-yearly sittings held after Michaelmas and after Easter, which all residents of the manor were obliged to attend. Interestingly, Edward was excused attendance at Michaelmas sessions in 1648 and 1649. The reason for his absence would be conjecture, but it is worth noting that these were the years of the Second Civil War, one of three wars collectively known as the English Civil War, a series of armed conflicts between Parliamentarians and Royalists, and the culmination of the constitutional problem I mentioned earlier. Although the war did not greatly impinge on the Salisbury district, the city itself was occupied in turn by both Royalist and Parliamentarian armies during the winter of 1644.

In 1662, just two years after King Charles II ascended to the throne following the collapse of Cromwell's Protectorate, Edward married Margaret Whitmarsh who lived in Salisbury Close, in the Cathedral precinct. She was the daughter of William Whitmarsh (junior) and his wife Dennis (then a fairly common name for females), and she was christened at Coombe Bissett in 1636. When they married, Edward was about 34 and she was eight years younger.

Marriage Bonds and Allegations were prerequisites if a couple wished to marry by licence rather than by banns. The bond affirmed, in language still familiar today, that there was no moral or legal reason why the couple could not be married. Interestingly, it also affirmed that the groom would not change his mind: if he did, and did not marry the intended bride, he would forfeit the bond. The groom, or a brother or uncle to the bride or occasionally the bride herself, and not necessarily a parent, was required to stand surety, 'bonded' for a fairly large sum of money jointly with the relative. The bond supported the *bona fides* of the formal statements in the application for a licence, and if the groom defaulted on the marriage plans the sureties would forfeit the bonded sum of money.

So following this procedure, Edward entered a marriage bond with

William Whitmarsh as his fellow bondsman. The following year Edward returned the dubious compliment by acting as bondsman for Margaret's sister, Elizabeth. The Act Book of the Dean of Salisbury contains the request dated 6 May 1662 for the marriage licence of Edward and Margaret. It named Edward as a husbandman of Coombe Bissett, and gave his age as 34 years or thereabouts; Margaret's age is given as 26 years or thereabouts, and they were said to have their parents' consent.

Edward and Margaret had six children: Edward, christened in 1662; William, christened in 1664 who died a bachelor in 1741; John, christened in 1666; Richard, christened in 1668 (I believe Richard had two daughters called Mary and Dennis, and that he died in 1702); Christabel, christened in 1670, who died just nine years later; and Dennis (a daughter), christened in 1675 and believed to have died in 1717.

Edward died in 1681 and Margaret died in 1696.

Crossing county borders

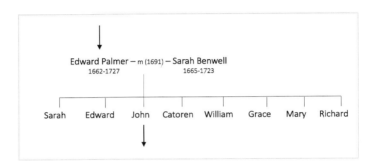

So in 1662, soon after the monarchy was restored, yet another Edward Palmer was born to Edward and Margaret, and this one was my great-great-great-great-great-great-great-grandfather. He too was a yeoman in Coombe Bissett. In 1691 at West Harnham, Salisbury, he married Sarah Benwell, three years his junior. She hailed from Oxenwood, near Shalbourne on the county border between Berkshire and Wilshire: at twenty-eight miles north of Coombe Bissett, Oxenwood was some distance in those times.

Edward's father-in-law, John Benwell, died in 1715. John Benwell's Will refers to Sarah, and also her (and Edward's) children Sarah and John; it also mentions a 'Grandmother Basin', who is believed to have been Mr Benwell's late mother-in-law, and the reference is perhaps to her as a member of the Bassing family of Shalbourne, rather than to a kitchen utensil!

Edward and Sarah had eight children:

The first child, Sarah Palmer, was born in 1691 or 1692. She married Philip Fort at West Harnham in 1715, and they had four children, Stephen, Sarah, Philip and Edward.

The second child, Edward Palmer, was born in 1693. He married Dennis in 1741, but she died the following year. Edward died in 1773.

The third child, John, was born in 1695 and christened at Shalbourne. Two years later a fourth child, Catoren, arrived.

The fifth child, William, was born in 1699. He was an ostler (a stableman at an inn), and in 1733 he married 27-year-old Margaret Lanham, the daughter of Joseph Lanham, an innkeeper from Melksham. William and Margaret had six children, the first of whom was born three months after their marriage. When his older brother Edward died in 1773, William inherited his house, land and other premises leased from Lord Londonderry in Coombe Bissett. Then when William died it passed to his widow Margaret; she had already been the heir to part of the estate of her brother Joseph Lanham junior in 1770. Margaret died in 1794 leaving bequests to her five surviving children, including one named Betty to whom she left the leasehold estate in Coombe Bissett and a share of a house in Salisbury. She also left bequests to the children of a son who had predeceased her.

Edward and Sarah's sixth child, Grace Palmer, was born in 1701 and died when she was seventeen. Their seventh child, Mary Palmer, was born in 1703, the year in which a great storm destroyed many properties in Wiltshire. Mary married William Barber: yes, one of those Barbers I mentioned earlier. The eighth and last child, Richard, was born in 1706.

Sarah died in 1723, and Edward died in 1727, the same year as King George I and Isaac Newton. Edward was buried at Coombe Bissett church on 19 August 1727. In his Will he appointed his son Edward to be Executor, and left 40 shillings to Edward; that's about £170 today but then was about 20 days' wages for a craftsman. Edward also left various items of furniture and 30 shillings to his daughter Mary, a pewter dish to his daughter Sarah Fort, and 20 shillings to his grandson Steven Fort (picture 4).

A wife with an inheritance

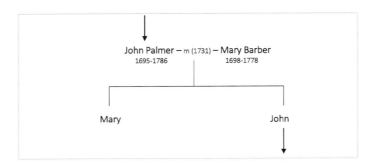

*E*dward and Sarah's third child, John Palmer, was my great-great-great-great-great-great-grandfather.

John was born in 1695, shortly after King William's young queen, Mary, had died of smallpox. In 1731 John was married by licence to Mary Barber, three years his junior.

Mary's uncle, John Barber, had been the innkeeper at the Fox and Goose in Coombe Bissett, as was his son (Mary's cousin) John. We might today consider it a contradiction that this innkeeper also registered his home as a Dissenters' Meeting House: Protestant believers who formed congregations outside the Church of England were commonly referred to as dissenters or non-conformists, and they would gather in meeting houses. The Act of Toleration in 1689 allowed them to have freedom to worship in this way, but required them to register their meeting houses with the local Quarter Sessions, the bishops or the archdeacons. John Barber duly registered his house in 1710: this was perhaps the first reliable evidence of non-conformism in the family, which later was to develop into a firm attachment to Methodism.

Mary had inherited from her father a tenancy in Lord Arundell's manor of Ansty. Henry 8th Baron Arundell of Wardour was a nobleman and a staunch Roman Catholic. An avid collector of art, he accumulated immense debts in building and furnishing New Wardour Castle near Tisbury, about twelve miles from Coombe Bissett.

In 1733 Mary and John had a daughter also called Mary, who in 1766 married David Feltham and themselves had a daughter called Mary.

In 1736, Mary and John had a son, another John I regret to say.

Mary died in 1778, and her tenancy passed to her husband. John died eight years later in 1786. They are both buried in Coombe Bissett churchyard.

A generous uncle

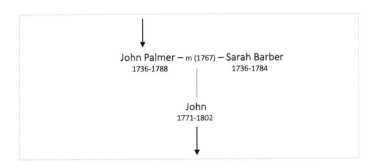

*I*n 1736 Parliament legislated in an attempt to curtail the consumption of gin, there were riots in London protesting at Irish immigrants providing cheap labour, and John and Mary's son John was born. He was my great-great-great-great-great-grandfather.

John was born in Coombe Bissett on 30 May 1736. He was a yeoman, and in October 1767 he married his cousin Sarah Barber, who was the same age. In 1771 they had a son, yet another John.

In 1773, he inherited from his uncle, Edward Palmer, property and a granary that stood on Edward's leased estate in Coombe Bissett, together with the residue of his goods and chattels after specific bequests. The Will (picture 5) said:

> *I give unto my nephew John Palmer, son of my said brother John Palmer, all that my reekhouse and granary adjoining together now standing ….. All the rest and residue of my goods and chattels, ready money securities for money rights credits and personal effects whatsoever (my debts legacies and funeral expenses being first paid and discharged) I give and bequeath unto my said nephew John Palmer, whom I do make sole executor of this my will.*

Sarah died in 1784, and John died in Coombe Bissett in 1788.

At this juncture it is perhaps worth pausing to reflect on the status of the Palmers – or at least the Palmer men – in the village of Coombe Bissett up until the end of the eighteenth century. They clearly had considerable status as yeomen, holding office within the church and the manor, and were well-respected: they witnessed the Wills and valued the assets of their neighbours. The community was well-structured, and the Palmers would no doubt have been viewed as leaders.

The Palmers were hardworking people, and although one would not class them as wealthy the likelihood is that they were comfortable compared with many at the time. They would have worked a number of strips of land and John, having inherited from his uncle, also leased land and a house from Lord Arundell. In addition, he held copyhold in the half-manor owned by Winchester College, and a further two copyholds in the half-manor owned by Lord Radnor. It is possible that he also owned some freehold land. In addition, he had the right to graze fixed numbers of sheep and cattle on Coombe Bissett Down, where to this day the visitor can still see the 'strip lynchets', the mediaeval terraces cut into the slopes to create arable fields.

This then was the situation that prevailed and had developed over perhaps six centuries. But the coincidence of personal tragedy and an Act of Parliament would soon transform the family's circumstances.

Two young orphans

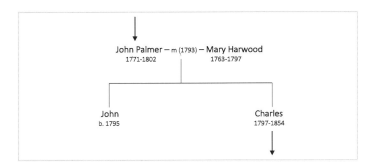

So the latest John Palmer was born in Coombe Bissett in 1771, and he was my great-great-great-great-grandfather.

In December 1793 John married 30-year-old Mary Harwood in Stratford Tony; the Harwood family came from there, and several – including Mary's parents – are buried in the village churchyard. As well as being a large family, it was also an unfortunate one: in 1809 a William Harwood was killed when his horse rode into a post, and eleven years later a Robert Harwood was found dead in a river after his horse returned home without him following a ride to Salisbury.

John's marriage to Mary joined the Palmers not only to the Harwood family, but also to the Meaden family. In 1778, Mary's sister Elizabeth, known as Betsy, married Samuel Meaden of Coombe Bissett, who was both a master carpenter and a master wheelwright. A painter (a craftsman, rather than an artist) called William Small wrote about Mary's nephew (Samuel's son) Charles Meaden. Mr Small's story tells a little about the family and their way of life:

Mr. Charles Meaden, wheelwright etc of Coombe Bissett. About the year 1829 or 1830 my father became acquainted with him and he used to say he wished he had known him before, he could have done him a great deal of good. My father painted waggons and carts for him and marked them. Mrs Meaden was a kind woman and her only beloved daughter Elizabeth was taken away from them in the year 1837, aged about 19 or 20 years, which was a great blow to them. I used to go with Father when a boy to help him, and have good things to eat and drink, they were very happy homely people and the property was their own. Mr. Meaden's cider was most excellent and to see my Father and him having a pipe and the two-handled cup sometimes, and Mrs Meaden and her lovely daughter sitting there too, it was a sight precious to memory. And Mrs Meaden were not long apart, about the years 1850 or 1851 they died. Mr Spicer, a worthy man that worked for them a number of years, had the business. Mr Meaden paid my father a bill once in spade guineas, 3 or 4 of them. it was a dark december saturday night about half past seven o'clock and when we came to Coombe turnpike, by the light of the oil lamp, he took the money out and put it in his watch pocket, saying that the robbers would not find it, for the roads at that time were not by any means safe.

John and Mary had two sons. The first, John (yes, another one!), was born in 1795. His brother Charles was born in 1797, but on 30 August of that year, the day on which author Mary Shelley was born, Mary Palmer died, possibly in childbirth. She was buried in Coombe Bissett churchyard.

Mary's widower John was left to care for the two boys, but it seems likely that at the end of March 1802, when he signed his Will (pictures 6 and 7) making provision for his two young sons, he was very ill and knew that he did not have long to live. He died just 22 days later, on 22 April, and the two boys were orphaned at the ages of just seven and five.

In his Will, John left his freehold, leasehold and copyhold property to be held in trust for the two boys for their maintenance, education and support until they reached the age of 21. The executors were John's friend George Sandy, an ironmonger, and Thomas Oakford, a 'gentleman', both from Salisbury. The accounts (picture 8) prepared by John's executors show that Charles Meaden's father's carpentry skills were put to use when his uncle John Palmer died: Samuel Meaden made his coffin, at a cost of one pound fourteen shillings and two pence. They also record payments to the coffin bearers, while other costs relating to the funeral include cloaks, black cloth, a shroud, tea, 'biscakes', sugar, wine, beer, sherry and a neck of veal. It seems that John was given a fine send-off. The detailed accounts also give some insight into the way the family lived and worked. John, Mary and the two youngsters lived in a house with a kitchen and three bedrooms, which was well-stocked and furnished. The farm stock included carthorses and a wagon, fowls, 15 ewes and lambs, and a dog. The land included around five acres each of wheat, barley and oats, together valued at around £56. The auction of all of John's assets raised £218, equivalent to around £7,000 today.

During the eighteenth and nineteenth centuries land was enclosed by means of local Inclosure Acts. These 'parliamentary' enclosures designated by Commissioners consolidated strips in the open fields into more compact units, and enclosed much of the remaining pasture land. The enclosures usually provided commoners with some other land in compensation for the loss of common rights, although it was often small and of poor quality. Some people benefitted, notably the key landowners, who made large profits from enclosures because the new fields were more efficient and they could charge their tenants higher rents. Some tenant farmers benefitted too: they did not mind the higher rents because they were making so much profit that they could afford new machinery and the best fertiliser. And some general labourers benefitted, because they were given more work digging ditches, planting hedges and building roads, while many even gained new homes on their master's estates.

But if some were winners the majority were losers, such as those smallholders who lost their land and were forced to become labourers, either because they could not prove their right to enclosed land, or because they could not afford to enclose land, while landless labourers, such as squatters, really suffered because the common land was turned into enclosed land, and many of them were left hungry. There is no doubt of the impact on Coombe Bissett and its inhabitants: village life changed hugely, and the context was established for the next generation, when the Palmers were destined to be simple agricultural labourers with no status, at the mercy of the job market and having to go wherever they were hired.

John Palmer's Will required his executors to sell and dispose of all his property. As he died in 1802, it is likely that his holdings were disposed of before the Act came into effect in 1806. I cannot say how the enclosure process emanating from the 1802 Act would have impacted on the sale of property at a time when it was being divided up and re-allocated by the Commissioners, but the crucial point is that the village environment within which those two youngsters would have been raised, together with their own prospects, was irrevocably different from what it had been during their father's lifetime and for generations before that. Nor do I know the detail of how the two young boys coped after their parents died, but the trust accounts include regular payments made to a Mrs Street for schooling. The concept of schools as we know them did not really reach Coombe Bissett until 1818, when the village clerk's wife conducted a school for 20 children, six of whom had their fees paid by the vicar. The lady of the manor supported another school, a Sunday and day school for 20 girls. The largest Sunday and day school catered for 28 boys and girls, and included children from other parishes. By 1858 boys and girls were also being taught in a roadside cottage in the parish. But even if he had a good education, it was certain that life would not be easy for John's children and the ensuing generations.

The family expands

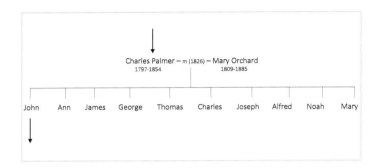

The younger of those two orphaned boys, Charles Palmer born in 1797, clearly survived being orphaned because he was my great-great-great-grandfather. On 20 July 1826, he married Mary Orchard at Coombe Bissett: Mary was just seventeen, twelve years younger than Charles.

In the aftermath of the Inclosure Act, life would have been difficult. In the year Charles married Mary, the journalist William Cobbett wrote about his journey from Warminster to Salisbury and commented on the poor living conditions of farm labourers. With plummeting salaries and grim conditions, Cobbett predicted - accurately as we shall soon see - that the discontent which he observed would lead to serious disturbances. It was only a few years later that the Poor Law Amendment Act of 1834, designed to reduce costs, stopped money going to poor people other than in exceptional circumstances, and said that able-bodied poor seeking relief must move into workhouses: during the following five years, fifteen new workhouses were constructed in Wiltshire whilst ten existing ones were enlarged. In August 1835, the *Salisbury and Winchester Journal* reported that at a local sheep fair which the Palmers might well have attended

> *... a great depression in prices was experienced. Ewes sold at a full six shillings less than last year, and lambs from six shillings to eight shillings [less], and many were driven home unsold ...*

Gone were the days when the Palmer men were yeomen and key members of the community. Now they were simple farm labourers in somebody else's employment, or working very small pieces of land. But seemingly undaunted by the economic difficulties, Charles and Mary produced ten children. The first, perhaps inevitably called John, was christened in November 1826: I shall return to him later.

The second child, Ann, was born in 1829. In 1851 she was employed as a housemaid by Elias Pitts Squarey who, aged just 27, employed 45 people at his 1,700-acre Manor Farm, Downton. Squarey went on to become rather more than a farmer: by 1873 he was a director of the Dorset Bank and the Small Farm & Labourers' Land Company, and was a renowned land valuer. Reporting his death in 1911, the *Western Gazette* wrote that he was

> *... one of the most famous land valuers in England. The greatest undertaking of his life was the purchase of sixty square miles on Salisbury Plain for the War Office.*

At Odstock Parish Church in May 1854, Ann married William Yeatman, a labourer. William and Ann each signed the Register with their marks, and one of the witnesses was John Hackett, a neighbour of Mr. Squarey. They had one son, Edwin, born in 1855. Ann died in 1902 having developed chronic rheumatism, and William died seven years later.

The third child, James, was born in 1831. At the age of twenty he was living with his older brother John and family in Coombe Bissett. James died at the Britford Union Workhouse in November 1876.

The fourth child, George, was born in 1834. When he was 17 he was still

brother Joseph. He remained a bachelor until he was 53, when he married Emma Everton, a widow who also lived in Homington, at the Primitive Methodist Chapel, Salisbury. An agricultural labourer, Noah's job was as a drowner on the water meadows: these were grass fields, usually beside a river, where water is made to run evenly across the surface so that the irrigation improves the grass and hay yields. They were operated by experts called 'drowners', because they drowned the grass. Water meadows around Coombe Bissett were part of an extensive system that had been constructed along a four-mile stretch of the river two centuries before Noah worked on them. Noah died from heart disease, dropsy and gangrene of the foot in February 1908 at 'Belmont', Coombe Bissett; he was 61.

The tenth child, Mary Sarah, was born in 1848.

By 1851, Charles and Mary's three older children had left home while the other seven were still living with them. George, Thomas and twelve-year-old Charles were working as agricultural servants, while Alfred and Joseph were at school.

Charles and Mary's family home at Shepherd's Close Cottage is still standing and is a listed building, but is now known as Jake's Cottage. It had once been the property of Charles' father's cousin Mary Feltham.

In the spring of 1854 Charles was taken ill with consumption (tuberculosis of the lungs), and he died in October having been ill for six months. His sons George and Thomas, both of whom died in their twenties, are buried with Charles in Coombe Bissett.

Later in life Charles' wife Mary lived with her younger half-brother David Feltham, a substantial farmer in Coombe Bissett with land all over the parish, including the plot just behind Shepherd's Close Cottage. David Feltham, described in the local press as '*highly respected*', died aged 80 in 1862, leaving amongst other bequests £5 '*to the widow of my late servant Charles Palmer deceased*'. So it was David Feltham who employed Charles Palmer as a farm labourer. David Feltham was not himself related to Charles, since it was David Feltham's father's first wife who was the Palmer, but he seems to have been a kind employer. Indeed, also in David Feltham's Will was a bequest to fund a donation of bread to the poor of Coombe Bissett every 18 December in perpetuity.

Mary outlived her husband by thirty years and died in Coombe Bissett in June 1885. The cause of death was recorded as 'old age': she was 76.

12

Spreading wings

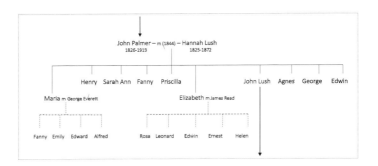

Charles and Mary's first child John, born in 1826, was my great-great-grandfather.

On 14 October 1844, when he was 18, John married 19-year-old Hannah Lush at Homington Church. The name Lush was to feature in the Palmer family over the next couple of generations. John and Hannah were young, but until 1929 boys could marry from the age of 14 and girls from 12, provided permission was received from the parents.

At this point, I should mention some significant events occurring in the world of agriculture that must have impacted on the family. In the second half of 1830, following a particularly poor harvest, agricultural labourers across Southern England, and notably in Wiltshire, protested about the hardships they were suffering, and specifically about the introduction of new threshing machines that were seen as the cause of unemployment. The protests were known as the Swing Riots, named after a fictitious Captain Swing, who 'signed' warnings and threats of action. Across Wiltshire labourers protested at food shortages and smashed the new machines, including some at Pythouse, twelve miles from Coombe Bissett, where the local militia dispersed a mob, killing one protester.

One of the landowners in Coombe Bissett parish, John Pinniger who owned Northend Farm, was a central figure in the November 1830 riots. His threshing machines had been destroyed and he had been attacked and robbed. Soon scores of rioters were apprehended and brought to trial. The names of some of those convicted at Salisbury Assizes in January 1831 are familiar, for Palmer and Lush feature in the list. A James Lush of Homington was found guilty of robbery, committed as part of a machine-smashing incident at Homington, and in April 1831 he was transported to Tasmania on the vessel *Proteus*. A Henry Lush was sentenced to death for his part in the riots, although after a public outcry and a petition his sentence was commuted to transportation. But despite the familiarity of these names and the likelihood that they were somehow related, I have not been able to positively identify them. Six years after the trials, the government pardoned almost all of the men convicted of rioting.

John's young wife Hannah was a servant. She was unable to write, and signed the marriage register with her mark, as indeed did the witnesses John Lucas and Marianne Lush. The Lush family hailed from across the county border, in Dorset. Hannah's father Henry Lush (almost certainly not the transportee), an agricultural labourer, was born in Fontmell, Dorset, in 1794. Henry was already living in the parish of Sixpenny Handley when he married his first wife Maria Green in November 1819. She was born at Tollard Royal in Dorset in 1801, so was still a minor in 1819: hence the wedding was *'with consent of parents'*. Their first child was christened six months later, on 24 May 1820.

Some of these place names are new to the reader, so I'll add a few words here about the geography. Sixpenny Handley, Woodcutts and Tollard Royal are neighbouring villages along a four-mile stretch of what is now the B3081 road leading towards Shaftesbury, and near the Wiltshire / Dorset county border. The villages are about nine miles from Coombe Bissett. King John's

House in Tollard Royal once belonged to General Sir Augustus Pitt-Rivers, known in Victorian times as the Father of Archaeology, and a soldier who had fought in the Crimean War at Sebastopol and Alma. This is one King John's House that, unlike most of that name, is believed actually to have associations with King John.

So Maria was Hannah's mother. Hannah was baptised in Woodcutts in March 1825. By the time Hannah was fifteen, her mother had died, Henry had remarried to Ann Cobb, and Hannah was living and working as a servant in Woodcutts.

Hannah's father Henry Lush remained at Woodcutts until at least 1861, and he worked as a farm labourer for William Wereat Perks, who eventually farmed 425 acres and employed 17 labourers at Woodcutts Farm, where Mr Perks lived with his wife, eight children, servants and a governess, while the labourers lived in neighbouring cottages. Between 1861 and 1871 Mr Perks moved to Winnall Farm, near the River Itchen at Winchester, which comprised 809 acres and employed 20 labourers and 6 boys. Henry Lush went with Mr Perks to Winnall. William Perks was a pillar of the local community: he was a church Guardian and a member of the Sanitary Authority, and by the end of the century he was living at The Friary in Southgate Road, Winchester and involved with the Soldiers' Home mission in Winchester High Street. He died aged 88 in Winchester in 1900, just a couple of years after his wife Ann; he left the equivalent of about £1.5m in today's money.

But I must return to John and Hannah who, like John's parents, produced ten children.

The first was Maria Palmer, born in 1845. By the age of 16 she was employed as a housemaid for local farmer George Brooks, who farmed 60 acres in Coombe Bissett. When she was 20, Maria married George Everett, a labourer and one of six sons from a farming family from nearby Great Wishford, although at the time of the marriage he was living in West Lavington: this was over twenty miles away from Coombe Bissett, but there is evidence that George had spent time in Coombe Bissett. Seven years later Maria and George, who was by then working as a shepherd, were living in Wylye, fourteen miles north-west of Coombe Bissett, with their young children Fanny, Emily, Edward and Alfred.

After Alfred was born in 1874, Maria and the family took the very big step of moving to the south-east of England: this was perhaps the first significant change of location for the Palmer family in their long history. When another daughter, Eva, was born in 1876 they were living in Sanderstead, near Croydon in South London. Within two years they had moved out to Sundridge, Kent, living at Chevening Park Lodge, where George was a stockman on Lord Stanhope's Chevening estate. While in Kent they had three more children: George junior born in 1878, Rosa born in 1880 or 1881, and Beatrice, born in 1882. Later Maria and George moved to Lewisham in South London, where George was a milk foreman. With them were Alfred, (now a milk carrier), George junior, Rosa and Beatrice. Maria Everett died in Croydon in 1934, aged 87.

John and Hannah's second child, Henry, was born in 1847 but died when he was just two weeks old having been 'weakly from birth'.

Their third child, Sarah Ann Palmer, was born in 1848.

The fourth child, Fanny, was born in 1851. In October 1868, aged just seventeen, she died of consumption and asthma in Cranborne, Dorset, after a three-month illness.

At this time John, Hannah and their children were living at Coombe Bissett in a cottage called 'Meadens'. John's younger brother James was also living there. John was a fervent Methodist: there was a Primitive Methodist chapel close to their home cottage, though it is possible that the cottage was attached to the chapel. Primitive Methodism was a working-class movement which began at the start of the nineteenth century, and quickly spread across England and beyond. It fired the hearts and minds of agricultural labourers, inspiring a passion for justice that led many to become leaders of the early trade unions. Primitive Methodism reflected a wish to return to the earlier and purer form of Methodism started by John Wesley in the eighteenth century.

John and Hannah's fifth child, Priscilla, was born in 1853. While a teenager she was an articled pupil, which meant that she was undergoing training but also had to work as a servant in return for the tuition. She worked at Stewart's Family Hotel in Sanatorium Road, Richmond Hill, Holdenhurst, near Bournemouth (picture 10). The hotel was formed when two large villas on Richmond Hill in Bournemouth, built by the town's founders Sir George Ivison Tapps and his son Sir George William Tapps-Gervis, were amalgamated. During the nineteenth century Stewart's Hotel was a firm favourite with Henry Fitzalan-Howard, the 15th Duke of Norfolk, and for him and his Duchess it was a regular summer retreat. Today the hotel is actually called The Norfolk Royale Hotel. By way of coincidence, an early ancestor of the Dukes of Norfolk was the first Earl of Arundell, a name the reader will recall from earlier chapters of this book. Arundel Castle in Sussex is the family seat of the Dukes of Norfolk.

Priscilla died at her sister Maria's home in Wylye in March 1873. She had suffered for twelve months from phthisis, a wasting disease, the most common form of which is pulmonary pneumonia. She died a year after her mother Hannah had died from exactly the same disease. Priscilla was just 19, and her sister Maria was with her when she died.

John and Hannah's sixth child, Elizabeth, was born in 1856. The records of this branch of the family are substantial, so I will devote rather more attention to them. Elizabeth left Wiltshire while still a teenager, and in May 1876 she was living in Croydon, where she married James Read, a carpenter and a Wiltshire man from Wylye. Her sister Maria and Maria's husband George were the witnesses. Medical records tell us not only that Elizabeth was pregnant at the time of the marriage but also that she had difficulty in getting James to marry her. Nevertheless it seems that, despite trying circumstances which I shall illustrate, he was well disposed towards her thereafter. Their first child was Rosa Matilda, born in Sanderstead, near Croydon, in 1876; the family then moved back to Wylye. Before Rosa was born Elizabeth had been a healthy, sober, and industrious woman; but then something happened that changed Elizabeth for the rest of her life, much of which she would spend in an asylum.

Mental health was not well understood in the late nineteeth century. The predominant approach at the time was one of institutionalisation, and many people with learning disabilities or mental health conditions were sent to asylums and other similar institutions to live apart from the rest of society. These institutions may to a degree have been places of treatment where people could be given specialised care, but they were mainly places of segregation and, to some degree, punishment.

The Wiltshire County Lunatic Asylum at Roundway in Devizes housed around 700 patients, and it was here that Elizabeth was admitted on 23 January 1877 (picture 11). Her medical notes confirm that she was '*suckling a child before admission*' – this would have been her daughter Rosa. Her admission to Roundway followed a week during which she been violent, breaking up furniture and smashing windows. Similar things happened while at Roundway, and she was often kept in solitary confinement. She would talk in a rambling manner, and could not give rational replies to questions. She was thin, emaciated and bad tempered. She was assigned to work in the laundry, which she seemed to enjoy. Eventually her condition improved, and she was discharged in May 1877.

There then followed a calmer period for Elizabeth and James. A year after her discharge she had their second child, Leonard Joseph Read, and over the next couple of years two more sons, Edwin Lush Read and Ernest James Read, were born (many years later, Ernest would marry his cousin, the daughter of his mother's brother John Lush Palmer). Then on 25 September 1890 Elizabeth gave birth to a fifth child, named Helen, known as Nelly.

When the national census was taken on 5 April 1891 Elizabeth's husband James Read was in Wylye with four of their children: fifteen-year-old Rosa was a housekeeper, thirteen-year-old Leonard was an agricultural labourer, and Edwin and Ernest were at school. But Elizabeth's name did not appear on the census form. Nor did that of the baby Helen. This was because Elizabeth had been readmitted to the asylum in October 1890, just a month after Helen was born. Her name appeared instead in the census of patients in Roundway, she being described as '*a lunatic*' and '*the wife of a carpenter*'. In April 1891 the baby Helen was being cared for by the family of her uncle, George Shergold.

This time in the asylum Elizabeth was alleging that she was not in fact married, and that she would have drowned herself if she could. She was violent at night, '*calling for pistols and dressing up for a ball*', and in October 1892 she was described as '*restless, excited, talkative and abusive*'. She was '*carrying on all kinds of antics*', and it is said that she had lost affection for her child – presumably the young Helen. Although after a further twelve months she was no longer considered suicidal, she was still using foul and blasphemous language, was mischievous and noisy, destructive and very easily upset. But she was working well in the laundry and by 1895 she was '*beginning to evince a strong desire to regain her liberty*'. In June 1895, the doctors considered she was well enough to be discharged from the asylum (picture 12).

Sadly she was only at liberty for a few months, because she was re-admitted in October 1895 after her husband James reported that she had wandered about the bedroom at night using filthy language, that she dressed in his clothes, and that she abused her children calling her daughter '*a dirty bitch*'. Her former habits returned, as she used gestures and language considered '*filthy*' and was delusional. It was felt that she would '*soon require extra food to prevent exhaustion from the excitement*'. It seems likely that at the time of this admission Elizabeth was unaware that she was pregnant: her medical notes show that she aborted in the morning of 28 February 1896. The foetus appeared to have been dead for a week or two.

Over the following months and years, her condition and her behaviour followed similar erratic patterns. She was described as '*a most useful woman, noisy as before but usually harmless'*. But from time to time she had to be detained in seclusion, and on one occasion in 1898 after she smashed a window she had to spend fifteen seconds under a shower bath, a treatment (more likely a punishment) which was meant to deter bad behaviour, though her case notes suggest that she actually enjoyed the shower rather than learning from it. At that time the shower bath was the most prevalent device used to 'treat' the insane (and many physical ailments), and was to be found in every ward of an English public asylum.

By 1902, Elizabeth was alleging that her husband was the one that should have been sent to the asylum. By this time too she was described as seeming on the whole fairly happy: *'she has a sense of humour and is fond of horse play and practical joking'*. But in 1905 she was *'threatening to kill everybody in the place and thinking the night nurse was after her with a knife to stab her'*. Although at one point she asked when she might be sent home, her notes record that *'she seems really too well reconciled to asylum life'*. She once said that she was *'black all over and was in hell'* and could hear imaginary voices, and suggested that the staff were all talking maliciously about her and her husband. The notes also record that *'she knows the matron and charge nurse, but mistakes the junior nurses for her daughter and her niece'*.

By 1911 she was again saying that she should not be detained, but according to her notes *'she appears to have no real wish to leave the asylum'*. This was seemingly an accurate assessment, because Elizabeth remained at Roundway Asylum until she died from heart disease in October 1915. Her husband James survived her by six years.

Elizabeth's son Leonard warrants a mention. In 1894, he took a job in Trowbridge as a cleaner with the Great Western Railway, earning around three shillings a week. The company was to be his employer for the next 32 years. Although he climbed the career ladder through various grades of fireman and engine-man, his career was not without incident: he injured himself with a hammer while freeing a jammed coupling link (1899); he caused a derailment by not checking points properly (1906); he ran a car off the rail by reacting to a flag which was signalling another train (1906); he failed to notice that his train was running down a siding instead of the main line, and consequently ran into and damaged two coaches (1915); and he moved his train before the necessary hand-signal had been given, causing a collision and damage to rolling-stock (1926). Unsurprisingly, Leonard's eyesight was examined regularly, though perhaps surprisingly it was declared satisfactory. He was however cautioned following each of these events, and on one occasion his promotion was deferred.

Leonard Read married Bessie Pitt in her home village of Westport St. Mary, Malmesbury, in September 1900. His job took them to various addresses in Wiltshire, Somerset and Gloucestershire, and in 1901 they were living in Trowbridge. They had two children, Leonard and Violet Bessie, and in 1911 the family was living at Wollaston, near Stourbridge in Worcestershire. Bessie died in 1948, and Leonard died three years later in Barnsley Hall Hospital, Bromsgrove.

Elizabeth's son Edwin Lush Read, a baker, married Mabel Mitchell in January 1900 in Bromley, Kent, where they worked as bakers and confectioners. Their son Edwin James was born in 1901 in Bromley, and over the next decade they had four more children, the alliteratively named Eric, Enid, Ethel, and Elsie. Elizabeth's eldest child Rosa married William Shergold, a carter from Wylye, in 1922. He died in Warminster in 1947, aged 70. Rosa, who had lived at Fore Street, Wylye, died on 11 March 1959, aged 82.

Hannah's maiden name resurfaced when her and John's seventh child was named John Lush Palmer; he was born on 31 May 1858, and I shall return to him shortly as he was my great-grandfather.

Their eighth child was Agnes, born in 1860. By 1861, Hannah, notwithstanding that she and John had six children under fourteen living at home, was working as a laundress. The ninth child, George, was born in 1865. At the age of fifteen he was living with his sister Maria in Kent, but he died in Cardiff in 1885 from a combination of bronchitis and typhoid fever. He was nineteen years old. I cannot be sure why he was in Cardiff at that time but - as I shall shortly relate - his older brother John was by then well settled in the city, and George died at 3 Carlisle Street, which was about five minutes' walk from John's home. It seems likely that George had come to Cardiff with a view to finding work, possibly with John.

John and Hannah's last child Edwin was born in 1866. In that same year their landlord Thomas Harwood, the same farmer whose windows John's brother Joseph had vandalised, died. In his Will executed nine months earlier Mr Harwood directed his executors to sell the property in which John and his family lived, together with the properties either side which were rented by the Macklin and Ovens families. So the following year the properties were sold by auction and the family had to move on (picture 13).

John and Hannah set up home in the village of Martin near Fordingbridge, eight miles south-west of Salisbury. Today Martin is at the extreme western edge of Hampshire, but at that time it was part of Wiltshire. John and Hannah moved there with their young daughter Agnes and their three sons George, Edwin, and twelve-year-old John Lush Palmer, who was employed as a shepherd boy.

The attraction of Martin might have been that there were members of the Lawes family living there, or that there were a number of farmers employing labourers there. Another factor might have been that there was a Primitive Methodist preacher living in the village. The distance from Coombe Bissett to Martin was a relatively short, but it was a significant move given that – apart from some of the offspring – all the previous generations of Palmer had lived and worked in Coombe Bissett. Nevertheless, it was nothing compared to the change of surroundings and circumstances that was soon to impact on John Lush Palmer and, in time, his father John.

Hannah died at Martin in April 1872, aged 48; she had suffered from phthisis for several years. Louisa Dibbin, who lived in the village, was present when she died.

Hannah's father Henry Lush survived his daughter by three years.

He died at Winnall in March 1875, aged 76, of pleuro-pneumonia and exhaustion. Unusually for a labourer he left a Will, witnessed by his employer Mr Perks. After a number of other bequests, including his feather bed, bedding and clothes, he left one-third of the residue of his estate to Hannah's children, for them to inherit when the youngest reached the age of twenty-one.

In 1881 John was living at Bishopstone, two miles west of Stratford Toney, with his youngest child Edwin as his only cohabitant. Members of the Lawes family were living in the village, as were some Everetts, and given that Palmers had married into both of these families it seems likely that this factor led John and Edwin to the area. Nevertheless by 1901 it seems John was back in Coombe Bissett, and living alone. But Edwin's movements thereafter are a mystery. He doesn't appear in any UK census after 1881, and he does not seem to have married or died in the UK. There are a number of possibilities, the strongest of which is that he sailed to New York on the *City of Chicago* in October 1890, his destination stated to be Ohio, where he was naturalised as a US citizen nine years later. But although there are many records in the name of Edwin Palmer with similar birth years, including emigration and war service records, I have not been able to establish beyond doubt that any relate to John and Hannah's son Edwin.

Before I leave John Palmer I need to share a story that I firmly believe was indeed about him, although I cannot prove it beyond all doubt. The renowned English composer Ralph Vaughan Williams used to travel the country listening to folk songs that were only known and sung locally. He would then transcribe them in musical notation, and sometimes he would adapt and use them in his own compositions. On 1 August 1904 he visited the Fox and Goose in Coombe Bissett; he listened to a song called *The Waggoner* and subsequently transcribed the music (picture 14), adding a note in rather poor handwriting that reads:

Sung by a man called "Pardner" in the Fox and Goose, Coombe Bissett near Salisbury. He lived in a shepherd's (or drifter's) hut but he worked all the

*summer – went to London and other places in the winter, The Waggoner – I
doubt if I have this right except the chorus.*

The quotation marks around the name 'Pardner' were his, suggesting he
was unsure about the name. John would have had a strong Wiltshire accent,
and mistaking 'Palmer' for 'Pardner' is understandable and forgivable, and
I have not been able to find any person named 'Pardner' or 'Partner' living
in or near Coombe Bissett at the time. I learned from another descendant,
who was quite unaware of this event, that John was living in a shack – that
is, a hut; and although the reference to London might at first seem out of
place, the reader will recall that John's sisters Maria and Elizabeth had both
spent time living in South London and Kent, and it seems reasonable to
think that John might have gone to them in the winter rather than stay in
his shack. On the balance of probabilities, I am convinced that John Palmer
sang for Vaughan Williams, and contributed to his store of musical works.

At some time during the 1870s, John Lush Palmer took the momentous
decision to move from Coombe Bissett to Cardiff, escaping the poverty and
hardship into which he had been born and raised in rural Coombe Bissett
to face instead the industrial grime but economic hopes in South Wales;
and leaving his father John Palmer senior apparently alone in Wiltshire.

1. Church of St Michael & All Angels, Coombe Bissett.

2. The will of Edmund Palmer, 1598.

3. The will of Emma Palmer, 1598.

4. The will of Edward Palmer, 1727.

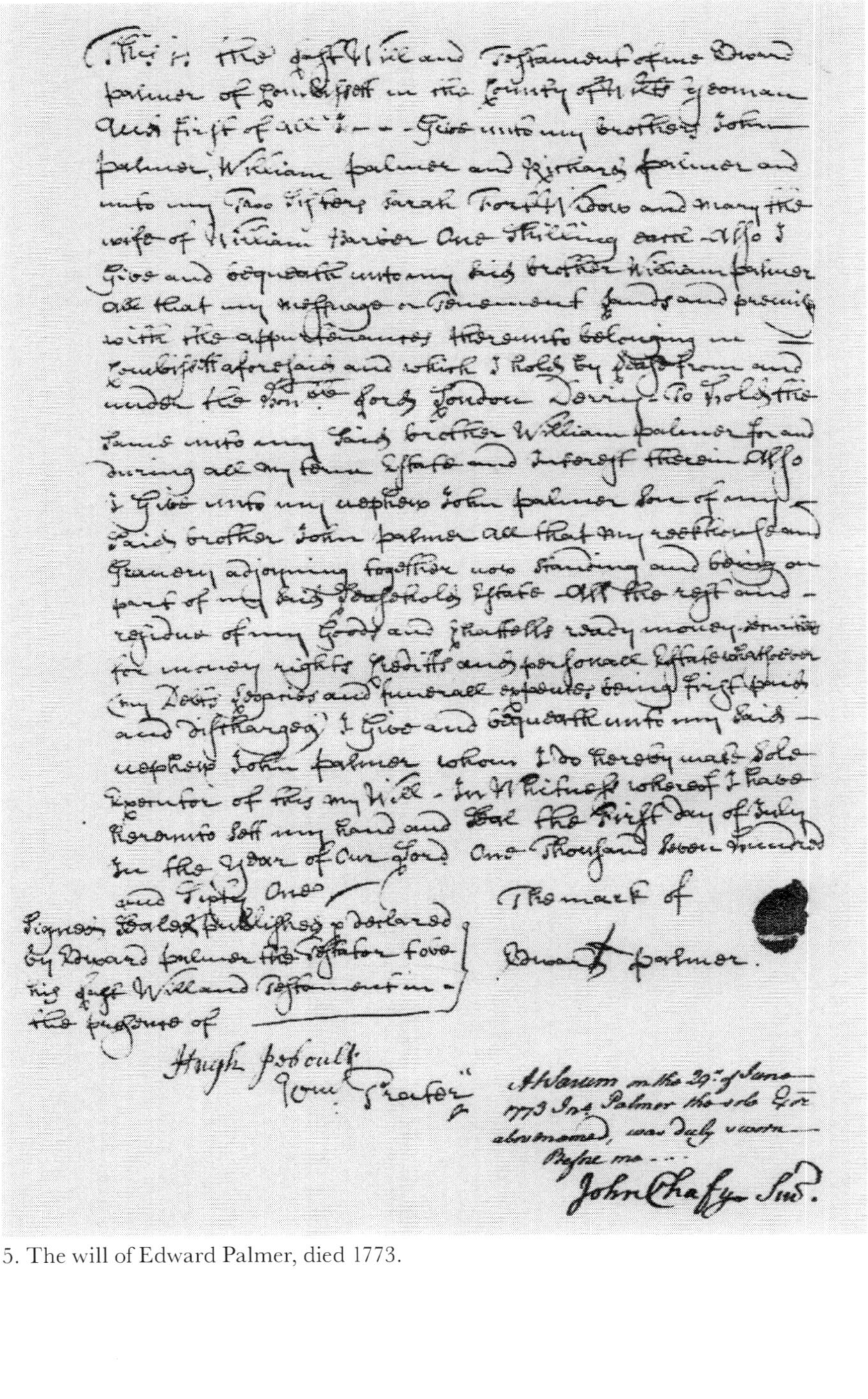

5. The will of Edward Palmer, died 1773.

This is the last Will and Testament of me John Palmer of Combe Byssett in the County of Wilts Yeoman, being of sound and perfect Mind Memory and Understanding praised be god for the same – I Give devise and bequeath unto my friend Mr George Sandey of the City of New Sarum in the County of Wilts Ironmonger and Thomas Oakford of the same City Gentleman All and Singular my freehold leaseholds and Copyhold Estates and all and singular my Stock of Horses, Corn, Grain & Implements of Husbandry, Household Goods and Furniture, Plate Linen and China Monies and Securities for Money and all other my Estate and Effects whatsoever and wheresoever and of what Nature Kind Description or Quality soever the same may be (save and except my Silver Watch hereinafter bequeathed to my Son John) To hold to them the said –

6. Extract from the will of John Palmer, 1802.

me at any time heretofore made and do declare this only to be and contain my Last Will and Testament In Witness whereof I have to this my Will contained in three Sheets of paper, at the bottom of the two preceding Sheets set my Hand, and to this third and last Sheet have set and subscribed my Hand and Seal this thirty first Day of March in the year of our Lord one thousand eight hundred and two –

John Palmer

Signed, sealed published and declared
by the said Testator John Palmer as and for
his last Will and Testament in the presence
of us, who at his request, in his presence, and
in the presence of each other, have hereunto
set and subscribed our Names as Witnesses

Robt Sede
John Flower
Benjn Sipps

7. Signature of John Palmer on will, 1802.

8. Extract from inventory of assets of John Palmer, 1802.

9. Report of the trial of Joseph Palmer, Salisbury & Winchester Journal, 2 April 1859.

10. Stewarts Hotel, Bournemouth.

11. Elizabeth Read, 1895.

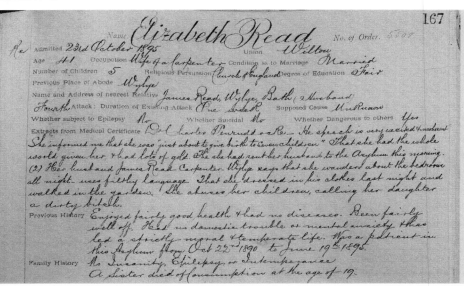

12. Extract from Elizabeth Read's case notes, Roundway Asylum, 1895.

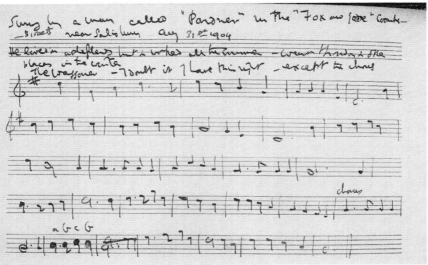

ON THURSDAY NEXT.
COOMBE BISSETT,
THREE MILES FROM SALISBURY.

MR. JOHN WATERS will SELL by AUCTION, at the FOX AND GOOSE INN, COOMBE, on THURSDAY, 16th MAY, 1867, at Four o'clock, by order of the Devisees of the late Mr. Thomas Harwood,—

THREE TENEMENTS AND GARDENS,

Situate at Coombe Bissett, containing about 12 perches, held by lease under Lord Folkestone for two healthy lives, aged respectively 22 and 14 years, and now in the occupation of John Palmer, George Macklin, and Charles Ovens.

MESSRS. WILSON, THRING, & NODDER,
9827]   Solicitors, Salisbury.

13. Sale notice for John Palmer's cottage, Salisbury & Winchester Journal, 4 May 1867.

14. Ralph Vaughan Williams' manuscript & notes, 31 August 1904.

15. Wharton Street, Cardiff, approx 1900.

16. 37 Sanquhar Street, 2014.

17. Notice of sale of 23 Coveny Street, Western Mail, 17 February 1894.

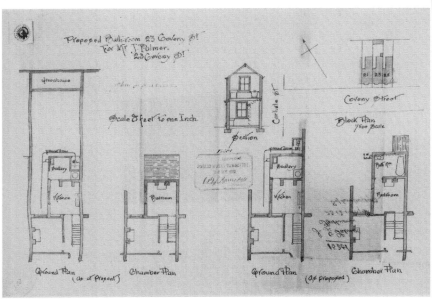

18. Plans of 23 Coveny Street - application for permission to add a bathroom, 1903.

Cardiff. Roath. R^d. Splott R^d.

James House.	55 Splott Road
Albert Palmer	23 Coveny Street Cardiff
Mary Ellen Bickell	77 Marion Street Cardiff
John Boadley	41 Splott R^d Cardiff
Edward Gifford	13 Railway St. Cardiff
Thomas Higgins	46 Aberystwith se Cardiff
Emma Palmer	23 Coveny Street Cardiff
Edna Smith	64 Splott Road Cardiff

19. Extracts from the Millennium Fund 'Historic Roll', 1898.

20. Windsor Terrace, Ely, approx 1900.

21. Ely Wesleyan Church Band of Hope.

22. Appointment of Ted, Walter and William Palmer as church trustees, 1930.

John L Palmer
35 Windsor Terrace Ely Cardiff
Market Gardener.

23. Signature of John Lush Palmer on a Methodist Church deed, 1916.

24. The family, approx 1910: l-r: back: Alfred, William, Fanny, Albert, Edwin.
Centre: Emma, Amelia Lucy, John Lush, Clara.
Front: Walter, Herbert.

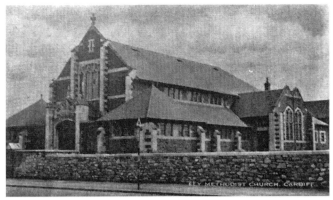

25. Ely Methodist Church.

26. Foundation-stone laying ceremony at Ely Methodist Church, 1910. Amelia Lucy Palmer is at the front, wearing a fur stole and large hat.

27. The Palmer sons, probably pre-World War 1. L-r: William, Herbert, Edwin, Albert, Walter, Alfred.

> **(2)** From Mr. J. L. Palmer, 35, Windsor-terrace, Ely, Cardiff:—
>
> " I am enclosing a cheque for £5 for your noble institution as a thankoffering to Almighty God for giving us victory over our terrible foes and for bringing my five boys through this awful struggle in safety. I only wish I could make it £50,000 instead of £5, but am thankful I am able to contribute my mite, in the hope that many more will follow my example."

28. John Lush Palmer's letter to Western Mail, 28 November 1918.

29. J Palmer and Son advertisement.

30. J Palmer and Son, company letterhead, 1942.

31. Harvesting onions, 1917. The group of four on the left are Ethel Irene Jones, John Lush Palmer, Ernest Beard & William Palmer. On the far right is Albert Sidney Jones. The man in uniform is believed to be a German prisoner-of-war assigned to work at the nurseries.

13

One giant leap

So John Lush Palmer travelled to Cardiff, doubtless taking the Great Western Railway train from Salisbury, albeit only for part of the journey because the GWR was not fully linked to Cardiff until the Severn Tunnel was completed in 1886.

In those days, a permanent move to an unfamiliar place over a hundred miles away was very significant – although many thousands of people did it. We cannot know for certain why young John decided to quit the agricultural life in rural Wiltshire, where he and his ancestors had lived and toiled for many centuries, and move to a big industrial city: but it can probably be explained by the contrast between agricultural decline and industrial growth over the second half of the century.

Between 1830 and 1880, the proportion of grain imported into Britain from abroad soared from 2% to 45%, while the price of British-grown corn fell by almost half, and while a million fewer acres of land were devoted to growing corn. Livestock farmers in Wiltshire also had difficulties: in 1835, the *Salisbury & Wiltshire Journal* reported that at one market

.... a great depression in prices was experienced. Ewes sold at a full 6s [shillings] less than last year, and lambs from 6s to 8s, and many were driven home unsold ....

The 1881 census showed a decline of 92,250 in agricultural labourers over the previous ten years, while the number of urban labourers increased to 53,496. Many of these had previously been farm workers who – like John – migrated to the cities to find employment, despite agricultural labourers' wages being the highest in Europe.

By contrast, in the nineteenth century Cardiff grew at a phenomenal rate. In 1801 the population of Cardiff was less than 1,900. By 1851 it was over 18,000, by 1871 almost 60,000, and by the turn of the century over 160,000. Exports of coal and iron from Cardiff and nearby Barry Dock boomed. Huge new docks were constructed to handle the trade, and the railway had reached Cardiff in 1841. The improved transport infrastructure fuelled further growth, and by the end of the nineteenth century Cardiff's industries included rope making, iron and steel, brewing, milling and paper making, while the town's docks exported more coal than anywhere else in the world.

But like so many other nineteenth century cities and towns Cardiff was overcrowded and dirty, and its infrastructure had not kept pace with its growth. Almost 400 people had died in a cholera outbreak in 1849. But there were improvements in the latter part of the century, when sewers were built and a piped water supply was installed. Public facilities improved hugely, but nevertheless the contrast with rural Wiltshire which John Lush Palmer found must have been tremendous, though I suspect that as a very young man he found the challenge to be as exciting as it was daunting.

14

Building the bricks

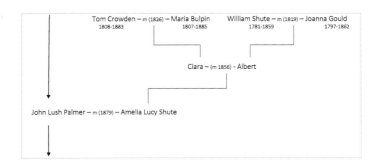

*A*t this stage I need to bring in two other families who, like John Lush Palmer, decided to leave their rural environment and seek to better themselves in the booming town that was Cardiff. These families both came from across the Bristol Channel in Somerset, and they were to be brought together by the huge demand for house bricks in Cardiff. Those two families were the Crowdens and the Shutes, and furthermore the business of brickmaking would eventually bring them to the Palmer family as well.

Tom Crowden was a brickmaker in Bridgwater, Somerset, but in the 1850s when he was around 40 years old he and his wife Maria and their eight children moved to Cardiff.

Albert Shute had been a labourer in a brickyard at the age of sixteen, despite the fact that the rest of his family worked in agriculture. The Shutes lived and worked in the small village of Pawlett, just four miles from the Crowden's home in Bridgwater, and around the time that the Crowden family moved to Cardiff, so did Albert Shute.

I shall now indulge in a little conjecture. It is quite likely that Albert knew the Crowdens, and highly likely that he was working with them. It is also distinctly possible that it was the Crowdens who encouraged Albert to move to Cardiff. Albert might have known the Crowdens' youngest daughter Clara in Somerset, but if he didn't he certainly became well acquainted with her in Cardiff, for they married on 27 October 1856 at St. John's Church in the heart of Cardiff. Clara was just eighteen.

Albert worked at Warings Brickworks in Rumney near Cardiff. He progressed well in the job, and was appointed foreman and eventually became owner and manager. The works supplied most of the bricks that built the masses of new houses necessary to keep pace with the city's inexorable growth in the second half of the century.

Albert and Clara set about raising a family, which would in time comprise nine children. Their first child, Amelia Lucy, was born in 1859 in a cottage on land that would eventually become the huge Dowlais Iron and Steel Works at East Moors, Cardiff. The second child, William, would follow in his footsteps in the brickworks, where he became a foreman. In later years a descendant of an employee who also worked there recalled the brickworks – and William Shute – as follows:

> *My father also used to tell me about the old brickworks. I can just remember the great ponds on Rumney Common where they used to dig the clay. I don't remember the names of them all, but there was a Waring's Brickyard, and as a boy my father worked there driving old Waring about in a little pony and cart. There was a big stationary steam engine driving the clay pugs and providing steam for the brickyard which was looked after by old Bill Shute, an old man with one arm. He had a hook for his other arm and my father and the other lads, wicked as they were, would root up the fire so that the old engine would blow, and old Bill Shute would chase after them trying to grab their jackets with his hook. One time when they were working in a clay pit, near where the power station now stands, there was a huge explosion and the flywheel of the old engine flew through the air and landed in the pit not many*

yards from where my father and his mates were working. I have heard many stories of the Brickyards, where they used to have thousands of bricks drying in racks, before being baked in the kilns. The sole drying agent was the wind, and there were shutters on the big drying racks with louvres that had to be altered every time the wind changed. The old people used to talk a lot about the hard winter of 1894/95 when the Rumney river froze and the frost went 4'6' to 5' into the clay and the brickyards couldn't work for about 15 weeks. That winter there was skating on the brickponds.

Around the time that Albert and Clara were having their fourth child in 1869, Tom and Maria Crowden were living at 30 Wharton Street, a stone's throw from the church where Albert and Clara had married. Tom kept a refreshment house, and they had a number of lodgers. Accommodation would have been much in demand, as skilled workers flooded into the town to take up the plentiful jobs in industry and commerce, and many lodging houses appeared in the town centre.

Wharton Street was originally a long thoroughfare from St. Mary Street eastward to the Hayes and beyond (picture 15). At various times in its history it had been called Broth Lane, Porrag Street and Porridge Lane. The road is still there, but has long since been enclosed by Cardiff's sprawling shopping centre, notably the department store James Howell. Along the road were, among others, a haircutter, a muffin baker, a fish and chip shop, while some years earlier there had been a slaughterhouse and the barracks of the Royal Glamorgan Militia. Wharton Street was close to Bethany Baptist Church (remnants of which still exist inside Howell's store), and many of the shops and cottages in Wharton Street were owned by the church. In the 1870s there were several public houses, including the Blue Anchor – which boasted a rifle range – and the Golden Lion, plus a tobacco factory, a school attached to the church, and some railway sidings.

And so it was that into this environment came John Lush Palmer at some time in the late 1870s. Either he found employment in the brickworks, and as a consequence found accommodation with the Crowdens in Wharton Street, or it happened the other way around. There were a lot of brickworks in Cardiff; although I cannot be sure, various factors point to the Grangetown Brickworks as being the site where John found work. Whichever it was, he soon got to know the Shute family, and especially their daughter Amelia. On 20 April 1879 at the same church where Albert and Clara had married 23 years earlier, 21-year-old John Lush Palmer married 20-year-old Amelia Lucy Shute. By this time Amelia's father, Albert, was manager of the brickworks. Albert, Clara and their children were living on the brickworks site. Clara's father, Tom Crowden, had retired and was living with Maria in New Wood Street, Cardiff.

15

Respectable tenants

*W*ithin a year John and Amelia had produced their first child, Clara, and had moved to 37 Sanquhar Street, Splott (picture 16). This curiously named suburb to the south-east of the city, close to the docks, was its industrial heartland, and it would be home to the Palmer family for the best part of the next two decades.

Splott epitomised the Industrial Revolution in the city, and it developed in line with the Revolution, largely as a consequence of the founding of ironworks. Splott transformed at an astounding pace, as houses, streets, shops, schools and hospitals emerged where there had once been marshland – the East Moors – leading down to the estuary. Much of this had occurred on the back of the production and export of iron: new railways being constructed across the world were built substantially from South Wales iron. The state-of-the-art Dowlais Plant, opened in 1891 when the 2nd Lord Bute granted a lease to the Merthyr-based Dowlais company with its revolutionary smelting methods, soon made the old-style ironworks obsolete, and its blast furnaces and chimneys would dominate the Cardiff skyline, and Splott in particular, for the next eight decades, spewing out phenomenal levels of pollution by day often shrouding the town in darkness with ash, soot and acrid vapours, and by night providing a spectacular show of the leaping flames and arcing sparks.

At the beginning of the 1880s, John was working in the brickworks. Two of John's fellow labourers, Edmund Read and James Hagate, were boarding with the family at Sanquhar Street. John and Amelia were still there when their third child was baptised at St. Mary's, Roath, in May 1884, though by 1889 they had five children and had moved to 7 Coveny Street in Splott. John was then working as a gas stoker. But it wasn't just the family that occupied this small terraced house, because in a number of editions during May 1890 the *South Wales Echo* carried a small advertisement that read

> *Black Minorca Eggs, 2s 6d for 13; splendid layers. Apply J. Palmer, No. 7, Coveny Street, Splotlands, Cardiff.*

His experience with livestock, albeit on a small scale, had probably led him to see chickens and their eggs as a means of generating extra income. Furthermore, having spent most of his life before the move to Cardiff working on the land, it was perhaps no surprise – despite now working and living in a heavily industrialised environment – that both he and Amelia were also taking more than a passing interest in horticulture. In 1892 they both won prizes at the Cardiff Flower Show, being rewarded with top three positions for vegetables as well as for cut and wild flowers.

The Palmers were described as *'respectable tenants'* who, with help from the chickens, paid rent of seven shillings and sixpence a week. John's occupation was then a fireman: not a firefighter as we might now call it, but more likely a stoker. By 1893 he was working as a gas stoker, almost certainly for the Cardiff Gas Light and Coke Company at its works in Penarth Road, Grangetown, Cardiff. There would have been a big recruitment campaign at the time, because in June of that year the *South Wales Daily News* reported that the company was erecting a massive new gas-holder. Until just three years earlier, gas stokers would have worked twelve-hour shifts, but a strike in South London eventually led to gas stokers working an eight-hour day. And action at the Cardiff company itself in 1890 led to the stokers being given a pay rise of 6d a week, though it was still argued that pay rates at Cardiff were lower than in other comparable cities; what is more the men were forced to abandon their additional demand for a week's holiday. Conditions must have been well-nigh unbearable: officials at the Cardiff site later admitted that workers had once toiled in dusty, dirty and confined conditions as they handled coal and ashes by hand.

Coal gas was prepared by distilling coal in huge fireclay retorts, and consisted principally of hydrogen and methane. Coal was loaded into the retorts, which were heated by the furnace, and the gas was given off. The gas stoker's job was to shovel the coal into the retorts, and later to take out the red-hot coke. As the fresh coal went into the burning retort it naturally caught fire: the stokers wore hats to protect their hair from sparks, but the environment was too hot to wear many clothes, and of course nobody even thought about trying to protect their lungs. John would have turned up for work every day knowing that he would earn his few shillings carrying flaming coal and breathing in the fumes, with the ever-present risk of being badly burned if anything went wrong. It was not a job for the weak, and accidents must have been commonplace. On 30 January 1902 the *Evening Express* reported that a gas stoker had been

> ... *severely burned at the Penarth Road Gas Works this morning. The unfortunate man opened the door of the retort in the ordinary way, and a considerable quantity of burning coal immediately fell upon him ...*

Working as a gas stoker must have been truly horrible for John, and the absolute antithesis of tending sheep on Coombe Bissett Down.

In 1893 John moved the family along the road to 23 Coveny Street (picture 17) paying eight shillings a week rent, and they were still there in 1901 with, by this time, ten children aged from twenty-one years to seven months old, namely Clara, Emma, Albert, William, Fanny, my grandfather Edwin (always known as Ted), Alfred, Walter and Herbert; the tenth was the baby Ernest, born in 1900, who sadly died aged just thirteen months after suffering broncho-pneumonia for three weeks.

Another child, Ivor Lush Palmer, had been born in 1893, but he died at 23 Coveny Street from *'vomiting exhaustion'* aged just 17 months.

Around this time 90% of properties were rented. A report by the Board of Trade in 1903 found that the typical urban labourer, earning 29s 10d per week, spent 22s 6d of it on food alone. Another study by Rowntree in 1900 found that a clerk earning 35s a week spent around 60% of his income on food. In other words, and unlike today, the proportion of total income spent on housing was relatively low. A typical labourer spent 3s a week on rent for three rooms, while a clerk paid 5s 6d a week for a house with five rooms, a scullery and a small flower garden.

But if their own back garden was a source of some pleasure, the Palmers' house at 23 Coveny Street was surely not! A small and overcrowded terraced house, it had one toilet off the kitchen, but no bathroom. In September 1903 John sought to rectify that by getting planning permission to have a bathroom added as an extension to the house (picture 18). Although by then Clara had married and left home, there were still ten people living there including offspring aged between five and twenty-two.

At least some of the children would have attended Splottland Road Board (Council) School, built around 1883. Life there could be tough: in November 1896 an assistant master from the school was summoned before the Magistrate for assaulting one of his pupils by striking him across the face with the cane. His defence was that it had been an accident, and the Magistrate sympathetically dismissed the case, although the prosecuting lawyer made it clear that if he had bothered to hear *all* of the evidence he would have concluded that it was in fact a very cruel case of assault.

But life at the school wasn't all bad. In 1904, the Government's school inspectors reported that '... *the school is carefully and sensibly taught and the children seem to be happy ...*', though it pointed out that '*… the babies' room should not be overcrowded …*' In 1908, Mrs Lloyd George, the wife of the then Chancellor of the Exchequer (and future Prime Minister), visited the school to present attendance prizes.

The Palmer family were members of the Splott Road Wesleyan Methodist Church. Lord Tredegar had laid the foundation stone, and had remarked that '*a great stir was now being made in endeavours to find out whether or not one religion could not be made to fit in with another*'. This was a time of considerable religious revivalism, and the Wesleyan churches were at the forefront. On 4 February 1905 the *Cardiff Times* reported unabated enthusiasm in crowded churches under the headline '*The Revival*'. It said that there was

> *… no diminution of revival fervour in the churches of South Wales … In scores of churches prayer meetings are held daily, being preceded in some cases by open-air services for the ingathering of people as yet unaffected by revival enthusiasm.*

Specifically the newspaper reported that

> *At Splott Road Wesleyan Church the revival is now in its fifth week. There has not been a single service without conversions. Last Sunday night they were 15.*

Cardiff itself had for some time been a focus for Wesleyan Methodism, and in the 'Circuit' within which it was located, covering half a dozen counties, the city's Methodist churchgoers accounted for a disproportionately high number of the total membership.

The Palmers' church was also ardent in its support for the Passive Resistance Movement and the Cardiff Progressives branch. The National Passive Resistance Movement encouraged nonconformists to oppose Prime Minister Balfour's Education Act, which provided funds for denominational religious instruction in Church of England and Roman Catholic schools, but no others. Opposition to the Act came especially from Methodists and Baptists, and contributed significantly to the Liberal Party defeating the Conservatives in the General Election in 1906. According to the *Cardiff Times* in April 1905, a senior official of the movement saw the Cardiff Progressives as '... *putting themselves in battle array* ...' when he preached at Splott Road Wesleyan Methodist Church.

Despite the financial struggles this large family must have faced, the Palmer children were contributors to the Wesleyan Methodist Twentieth Century Fund: in 1898, the Wesleyan Church launched an appeal to raise *'One Million Guineas from One Million Wesleyans'* to finance a huge programme of evangelical work and social action. The Palmer children's names appear on the Historical Roll, which means they each donated at least one guinea. The fund, which was known as *'The Million Guinea Fund'*, finally closed on 30 June 1904, having failed to reach its target in 1901. In the end it raised £1,075,727.13s.8d. The 17,000 pages showing the names of the donors were bound, and a special bookcase was commissioned and placed in Westminster Central Hall, London, following its opening in 1912 and this is where the Historic Roll can still be seen today (picture 19).

In 1904, John – suffering from chest problems as a result of his work in the heat and the fumes of the gasworks – moved with the family to Ely, a village to the west of the town. At that time it seems unlikely that John was able to buy the house in which they were to live or the land on which they were to work. He had access to some capital: around 1887 he would have received his legacy from his maternal grandfather Henry Lush, which could only be paid when the youngest of John's siblings attained twenty-one. However, the relevant one-third share of Henry's assets had to be divided between Hannah's children; Hannah gave birth to eleven children, and although a number had died there were probably half a dozen surviving when the legacies became payable, and between whom the money had to be divided. Henry left *'effects under £100'*, so the likelihood is that John's share was quite small.

Perhaps more significantly, in 1898 Amelia had inherited about £100 from her father which was payable on the death of her mother, and that was equivalent to about £6,000 today. Three of John's sons were of working age and would have supplemented the family funds. John had worked very long hours in a harsh environment to provide for his family and to keep a roof over their heads. Even so, this was a large family, and after rent of at least eight shillings a week in Coveny Street there would not have been much to save towards property purchase, even though in Ely land and property prices would have undoubtedly been cheaper than in the town itself.

But however it came about, just around the time that Cardiff had become a city John Lush Palmer had become a market gardener in Ely.

16

Back to the land in unsettled times

Until the turn of the century Ely, a few miles west of Cardiff, was no more than a small hamlet consisting of the few farmsteads, small clusters of houses, and some wayside inns near a narrow arched stone bridge that crossed the River Ely, which still flows south to the Severn Channel. The farmers and market gardeners in Ely supplied the food needs of a rapidly growing Cardiff, sending their horse carts along country roads that were said to be a terrible journey even on foot. Most of Ely was owned by the Earl of Plymouth, who dictated that alcohol should not be sold on the land. As a result the boundaries of the old estate can be approximated by the locations of public houses around the area.

John and Amelia and their children set up home at 35 Cowbridge Road, near the Plymouth Estate's eastern boundary. The property was at the end of a section of Cowbridge Road called Windsor Terrace, which ran west from the bridge over the River Ely. The Palmers lived in number 35, at the corner of what is now Colin Way (picture 20).

The younger children would have attended Ely Council Board School in nearby Clarke Street, now known as Millbank School. Ely was a village, and yet the nearby Ely Racecourse attracted huge crowds to its horse-race meetings, especially the annual Welsh Grand National which up to 40,000 racegoers would attend. The Palmers' religious beliefs might well have dissuaded them from placing bets, and given that for twenty years starting with their arrival in Ely the race was won by the same trainer, Mr. F Parker, the odds might have been fairly short.

In those early years of the century, development in the vicinity of the Palmers' homes and workplaces in Ely, around Cowbridge Road and later nearby Mill Road, was gradual. It kept pace with the expansion of the only real industrial sites, namely a brewery and a jam and pickles factory. And notwithstanding that Ely Paper Mills, just the other side of the bridge, was one of the biggest suppliers of newsprint in the world, Ely effectively remained a village until the construction in the 1920s of council houses to rehouse people from Cardiff's inner-city slums, following Prime Minister Lloyd George's call for *'homes fit for heroes'* after World War I. Perhaps as an inevitable consequence of its growth, in 1922 the village of Ely was brought into the Cardiff City Council boundaries.

The nurseries where John Palmer went to work, growing fruit, vegetables and flowers were known as Windsor Nurseries. A newspaper advertisement from before the turn of the century shows an *'E. Griffen & Co'* in business at *'Windsor Garden Nurseries, Ely'*, which was undoubtedly the same site as the nursery owned by John. Emma Griffin ran a florist's shop in Queen Street, in the centre of Cardiff, which is also mentioned in the advertisement, and her flowers were most likely grown at the Ely site. Emma didn't need to work: her husband was Henry Griffin, general manager of Cory Brothers & Co, who were colliery and shipping owners and the embodiment of commercial success in the boom town that was Cardiff. Nevertheless, the nursery in Ely was leased in his name and the horticultural tools in Ely were regarded as his property; indeed at Llandaff Police Court in 1885 a thief called James Taylor was committed to the Assizes for breaking into a shed in Mr. Griffin's garden in Ely, stealing tools, and then offering them for sale in a pub. But the loss of a few spades and garden forks would not have troubled Mr. Griffin unduly, for he was a very wealthy man. When he died in 1925, notwithstanding that Cory Brothers had suffered considerable setbacks because of the loss of most of their ships during the war, he left over £200,000.

Griffin leased Windsor Gardens from the Earl of Plymouth for an annual rental of £34.8s.6d. Although I can find no firm evidence, the likelihood is that John Palmer was working for the Griffins until 1917, when the Earl's accounts show that John took over responsibility for the lease paying £28.10s 0d a year, which was increased in 1919 by £3.10s.0d because he had taken over greenhouses previously owned by Mr Griffin. By 1920, John was paying £32 plus £8.8s 0d property tax to the Earl. This arrangement continued through until at least 1920. As for the name *Windsor Gardens*, the likely explanation is that the gardens were so named around 1883 when Lord Windsor of St. Fagan's (a village a few miles from Ely) married Alberta, daughter of Sir Augustus Paget. This theory is supported by the fact that the road adjacent to the garden site was then called Paget Road (or Street), which is now the aforementioned Colin Way.

Very quickly, and despite his recent arrival in the area, John became a leading light in the Wesleyan Methodist Church in Ely, which was then situated in Mill Road a few hundred metres from his home. Half a century later, the Church elders would write:

In 1904, a Godly man and his gracious wife settled in Ely with their family of six sons and three daughters. This was the Methodist family of Mr and Mrs John Palmer. They brought new vitality to the cause and were a tower of strength for many years. Playing vital roles in Sunday School, Band of Hope, Choir, Trust, and from time to time holding important offices in the Church ... It is a record worthy of note that in his lifetime Mr John Palmer was a founder-member of four Methodist churches. God has been pleased to bless His cause in Ely through the devoted and loyal families of men like ... Mr Palmer ... and we, their descendants, owe much to them.

As mentioned, the Palmer family were members of the Band of Hope, a temperance organisation for working-class children; all members took a pledge of total abstinence and were taught the 'evils of drink'. Members were enrolled from the age of six and met once a week to listen to lectures and participate in activities. In their parades, young boys wore 'Cadets of Temperance' uniforms and carried replica rifles, while the girls wore white dresses and carried flowers (picture 21).

Within a year of arriving in Ely, several of the Palmer children were Sunday School teachers, and soon John himself was Sunday School Superintendent. The names of John and his children appear frequently in the minutes of meetings from 1905 onwards. The family's ties to the Ely church would be strong for much of the twentieth century, and in 1930 Ted, William and Walter were appointed trustees of the church, and in due course trusteeship was passed to the next generation (pictures 22 and 23).

In 1909, the world's first one million pound cheque was written at the Cardiff Coal Exchange, while in the latter half of the year serious flooding affected the area around the Palmers' homes, as the River Ely, which flows close to Mill Road and Cowbridge Road, burst its banks. This was the second occurrence of serious flooding in fifteen months, and indeed it was to happen again in January 1918, when in Mill Road '… *the swirling water had reached to such a depth that it came up to a horse's stomach …*'.

In 1911, John was still at 35 Cowbridge Road with Amelia and six of their children: Clara and Emma had married and left home, and Ted had gone too (picture 24). Most of the family moved into houses in Mill Road, where John's son Albert, by then an accomplished bricklayer, was building new houses with his friend from childhood, George Pugsley. The Palmers, along with Amelia's sister Maria (known as 'Ri'), her husband Bill and their daughters Gwen and Olive, occupied a number of houses between numbers 48 and 58.

For Cardiff, 1911 was a difficult year and Home Secretary Winston Churchill sent 500 troops to the city to quell riots and race-related violence, which was directed primarily at Cardiff's Chinese community who were

on 30 August the *South Wales Echo* announced the death thus: *'PALMER –
On August 29th at the Priory Nurseries Langstone, Amelia Palmer aged 92. Late of Ely
....'* In the following day's edition, the words *'John, the beloved husband of'* had
been correctly inserted. One can imagine the dismay among family and
friends when they read the first notice!

John's Will, executed just a few months before he died, was witnessed
by the Reverend William Williams, who presided over his funeral at
Langstone. John's estate amounted to just over £4,500 – the equivalent of
about £180,000 today.

His remarkable story is worthy of a summary: John Lush Palmer was
born into the impoverished state that had beset the Palmer family since
the death of his great-grandfather at the start of the nineteenth century, a
state perhaps epitomised by the deaths of several members of the family
in workhouses and similar institutions. But rather than, Micawber-like,
waiting for something to turn up, he took the dramatic decision as a young
single man to move to the burgeoning city of Cardiff, where he laboured
resolutely in ghastly conditions to turn the family fortunes around, all the
while maintaining a steadfast devotion to God and His teachings through
the Wesleyan faith. Furthermore he returned to Wiltshire to rescue his ailing
father from his farmyard shack, reverted to earning the family income from
the land, and – as I shall describe in the next section – raised a brood of
children who would use an impressive array of talents to demonstrate the
same fortitude and resolve that he possessed.

Part Two : Challenges and Tragedies

John and Amelia's Children

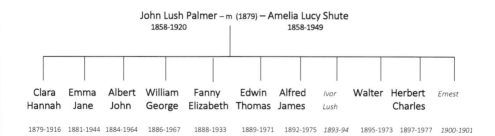

John Lush Palmer — m (1879) — Amelia Lucy Shute
1858-1920   1858-1949

Clara Hannah	Emma Jane	Albert John	William George	Fanny Elizabeth	Edwin Thomas	Alfred James	*Ivor Lush*	Walter	Herbert Charles	*Ernest*
1879-1916	1881-1944	1884-1964	1886-1967	1888-1933	1889-1971	1892-1975	*1893-94*	1895-1973	1897-1977	*1900-1901*

17

Torn apart

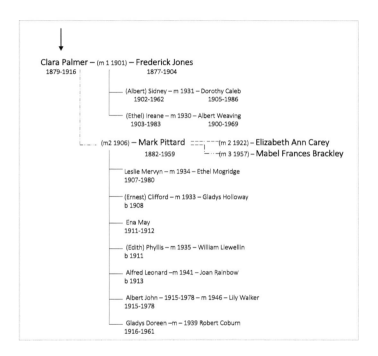

*C*lara Hannah Palmer was born in 1879. In 1901 when she was 22 she married stonemason Frederick Jones, and they had two children, Albert Sidney, known as Sid, born in October 1902, and Ethel Irene, known as Rene, born a year later. But when he was just 27 years old Frederick died at 98 Inverness Place, Cardiff. He had suffered from pneumonia for over a month, and contracted meningitis.

Just over two years later the widow Clara married 24-year-old Mark Pittard, who lived close to the new Palmer family home in Ely. In 1901, he had been working at the Ely Paper Works, though at the time of their marriage he was a brickmaker, and by 1911 a labourer in the Ely Brewery. Mark's family certainly knew hard times: in 1897, his nine-year-old brother Frank was found drowned in the River Ely, having been missing for three days. In the years towards the end of the first decade of the new century Mark's 60-year-old father John, who suffered from a variety of ailments, including heart disease and dropsy (which we now know as oedema), appeared in the *Paupers' List* as an outdoor pauper, meaning he was not living in an institution for paupers. In 1908 he received maintenance for himself, his wife and his children for 25 weeks at 8s a week, plus other payments including 8s for meat and 2s 6d for *'Christmas Relief'*. In total he received between £10 and £12 each half-year while registered as a pauper.

During World War I, Mark's younger brother, Albert Ernest Pittard, joined the Army Service Corps (Mechanical Transport) from the Reserves as a motor driver. He served for about two years, but his record suggests that he did not leave England. In 1917 he was assessed as permanently physically unfit. The origin of his medical problem was not known, though it was not the result of, or aggravated by, his service.

Clara's marriage to Mark resulted in a further six children born between 1907 and 1915, namely Leslie Mervyn, Ernest Clifford (known as Clifford), Ena May (who died aged just one year old), Edith Phyllis, Alfred Leonard (known as Leonard) and Albert John. Over that time the family lived in a number of houses in Mill Road.

Clara died at 32 Mill Road on 29 October 1916, three weeks after she gave birth to another child, Gladys Doreen. The birth had left her ill with pleurisy, and the death certificate gives the causes of death as childbirth and cardiac syncope (a sudden lack of blood supply to the brain caused by heart failure). She was just 37, and Mark, then a crane driver, was present when she died. I was told that he was a difficult and demanding husband, but even so it is hard not to sympathise with Mark, who was earning 39 shillings a week and was left a widower with six young children to care for

86

and maintain.

The new baby Gladys Doreen went to live with her aunt, Mark's sister Annie Adams, who also lived in Mill Road at number 2. Leslie, Leonard and Albert initially went to live with other relatives, but it soon became clear that even the family as a whole could not cope. John and Amelia were described by an official as '*very worthy Methodists hard pressed with the cares and troubles of the children of various parts of the family*', and as if to prove the point in January 1917 Leslie, Leonard and Albert were taken into an orphanage run by National Children's Homes (NCH). This was a charitable organisation closely associated with the Wesleyan Methodist church, and the family's intense and long-standing involvement with the church no doubt eased the way. Mark was required to contribute twelve shillings a week towards their care. Albert John went initially, and probably with his brothers, to Bonner Road Children's Home in Bethnal Green, London.

We next meet the Pittard children twelve years later, when Leonard and Albert, both still in care, were at an orphanage in Newcastle, and Leslie was in a home in Wadebridge in Cornwall, though he too had initially been in Newcastle for a short time after they were taken into care. Leonard and Albert expressed a wish to go to Canada.

Many youngsters were sent to Canada by the NCH under the child migration scheme. The migration had begun in 1873, when land and a home had been purchased with the assistance of local Methodists near Hamilton, Ontario. At first they sent both boys and girls to Canada but in the 1890s they stopped sending girls. The NCH estimated that about 85% of the children remained in Canada, while the other 15% either returned to England or went to the United States. The scheme had almost come to an end by 1929, and in 1928 the Canadian government had banned the immigration of children under the age of 14 who were not accompanied by their parents. So it is important to remember that Albert was approaching his fourteenth birthday, and that it was his decision to go.

Correspondence shows that as early as January 1929 both Leonard and

Albert were anxious to go to Canada. Their brother Leslie, in Cornwall, was informed that they were soon to sail to Canada, and on 11 February he wrote to the authorities ask if he could meet them '... *as this is 13 years now since we parted, and I would very much like to see them*'. He clearly felt a strong bond to the other boys, despite their long separation. Interestingly – and perhaps surprisingly – he added that '*it somehow seems our relatives do not seem to take much interest in us*'.

On 1 March, an Immigration Medical Card, valid until 1 July, was issued at Newcastle to Leonard (picture 33), and on 5 March NCH wrote to Leslie saying that his two brothers would be sailing on 16 March. Arrangements were made for the two boys to travel by train to London on 15 March to meet Leslie before they went to Liverpool, from where they would sail to Canada on the following day.

However, for some reason Leonard did *not* sail. Only Albert, who had been issued with a passport at Newcastle a fortnight earlier, is identified in the list of passengers who sailed from Liverpool on 16 March 1929 on the *SS Cedric*, along with 36 other boys aged 13-16, bound for Halifax, Nova Scotia. His brother Leonard's name did not appear in the passenger list, although it was on the Canadian Immigration Service's schedule of passengers arriving in Halifax on the *Cedric*. However his name has been crossed through and endorsed '*not on board*'. Indeed in July 1929 Leonard was still at the orphanage in Newcastle, but seemingly still keen to go to Canada. On 1 July, his Immigration Medical Card was renewed, and on 14 July he wrote to NCH Headquarters from the Newcastle Orphanage (picture 34) asking if he could now go to Canada, and stressing that his gardening skills had much improved '*since March*' and that '*... I can now do good work with the spade, and will do my best if I get the chance to go to Canada, and I want to be earning my own living ...*'

The implication is that a lack of horticultural skills might have been the reason why he was unable to travel with his brother, although this does not fully explain the sudden change of circumstances just before he was due to sail. In any event, in September 1932 still in England and in care, Leonard was placed with a Mr Whitmore in Arley, Coventry. In May 1933, NCH wrote to his uncles Albert and Herbert to say that Leonard, who by then was aged 20, had been '*the cause of very considerable anxiety*'. By 1939 Leonard was working as a machine grinder, and was living with in Wrigsham Street, Coventry with a family called Shelley.

The children who travelled from the UK were intended for permanent settlement in Canada; they were all described as '*adults*' in the passenger list, with '*farming*' as their occupation. Canadian immigration records show Albert Pittard's occupation in the UK as '*scholar & farming*', his intended occupation in Canada as '*farming*', and that along with others he was destined for an NCH orphanage at Fox Street, Hamilton. The entry under '*nearest relative's details*' simply shows '*NCH Orphanage*'.

Canadian Juvenile Inspection Records show that Albert worked for a number of different employers in the ensuing years. In May 1933, NCH reported that '*... he has done very well in Canada, though we have not heard from him since December 1932 when the report was excellent*'. One employer reported '*This boy is very hot-headed and sulks*', but adds that there were '*No complaints from Albert*' (picture 35).

There are some baffling issues surrounding the end of Albert's five-year stay in Canada. His final assignment was at Seaforth, Ontario, in 1934. In July of that year, Albert wrote to the authorities in Canada to say that he had heard from his sister in Wales that:

> *... my dad is still living, he was thought to have been killed in the war and he has never seen me. He has been suffering from loss of memory, and my sister wants me to come home. Her husband can give me a job on his farm .... dad and I has never seen each other yet. He was fighting overseas when I was born and my mother died shortly afterward and I was put in the home. I want to see my dad while he is living ... nineteen years is a long time for any father before he sees his son.*

There was some concern about finding the fare of $100, and he was advised by authorities in both Canada and England against making the journey. A NCH official wrote to Albert at the time to ask for an address for his sister in order to ascertain '... *if she is in a position to help you, and also enquire whether her husband is prepared to pay you wages in return for work on his farm ...*'.

This is perplexing, because in 1934 both of Albert's sisters, Edith Phyllis and Gladys Doreen, were single, and indeed there is no record that Albert provided NCH with any kind of response to their request for further information. Possibly he was referring to his step-sister, Irene, who was aged 31 at the time: we do know that she remained close to the family for many years. Albert had of course been taken into care as a baby, and was three when the war ended, so he would have no real memories of the war years. He was almost certainly wrong in saying his father had never seen him, because his father Mark was present when Albert's mother Clara died at their home in October 1916, and in January 1917 he had signed the agreement putting the three boys into care.

Albert's assertion that his father had wrongly been thought to be dead is also puzzling. Mark might have served in the latter half of the war, but no records have been traced. He had undoubtedly been living very openly in Cardiff since at least 1922, twelve years before Albert was writing that his sister had revealed that his father had not died in the war after all. One explanation might be that Albert was concocting a story in the hope of getting a paid passage home and, as will become apparent, might even have done so in collusion with his brother Leonard. That said, it is significant that when NCH wrote in May 1933 to report on Leonard, their letter was addressed to his uncles, not his father, which implies that Mark and the young men were in some way alienated, or that they were no longer in contact with their father Mark.

To add to the mystery, or perhaps to confirm one of those theories, Mark's details on the NCH form, which led to the boys being taken into the children's homes, have been crossed through and overwritten with the word '*deceased*'. The form remained in the custody of the NCH authorities. Mark did not die until the 1950s. It is highly unlikely that after so long, with Mark's sons themselves in middle age, some official would have so endorsed the form. Somebody must have told them.

In response to Albert's letter of July 1934, an NCH official warned him that '*... conditions in England are very bad at the present time, and unless you have a definite job to come over to here, you would be well advised to remain in Canada for the time being ...*' He was right: conditions in Britain were indeed very bad in 1934. It was the time of the Great Depression, when the unemployment rate was 25%. Areas of heavy industry (coal, iron, steel, shipbuilding) were most affected, and were already struggling because they had not modernised after the war and could not compete with other countries. Nevertheless, in August 1934 Albert did return to the UK from Montreal. In the same year South Wales, an industrial giant at the turn of the century and the home of Albert's family, was recognised in the Special Areas Act as one of the four regions with the worst socio-economic problems.

But Albert did not go to South Wales. He went straight to Coventry, where his brother Leonard had been since 1932, and in fact in 1939 Albert was lodging with a Mr and Mrs Gray in Longfellow Road Coventry, just a short distance from Leonard's home. Both Albert and Mr Gray were motor engine fitters.

Notwithstanding the Depression some parts of Britain, and some people, remained relatively affluent. As a consequence, sales of motor cars boomed; Coventry was one of the centres of car production, and indeed it was in the car manufacturing industry that Albert was to spend the rest of his working life. In November 1946 Albert, by then an electrical tester and inspector, married Lily Walker in Coventry. Albert died in Coventry in November 1978.

Mark Pittard had in fact been living in Ethel Street Cardiff since at least 1922, when he married Elizabeth Ann Carey, a 40-year-old widow, at the nearby St. Luke's Church, Canton, and he lived in Ethel Street until at least 1957. Elizabeth died in 1951, and Mark married for a third time in 1957, to 71-year-old Mabel Frances Brackley. But just two years later he died from chronic bronchitis and emphysema at his home at 10 Cornwall Street, Cardiff, aged 77. He had worked until the age of 70, most recently as a checker at the Cardiff Docks where he had earlier been a crane driver, and had outlived Clara by 43 years. In several of the family photographs in this book there appears a man with a large drooping moustache; although I cannot be sure beyond doubt, I believe that the man is Mark Pittard.

Clara's first child by her first husband, Sid, married 26-year-old Dorothy ('Dolly') Caleb in 1931. Sid was a wholesale fruiterer and florist; he and Dolly had two daughters, not twins although they were both born in 1933; first came Thelma, then Pamela. Thelma married William Sutton in 1956, while Pamela married Lawrence Wallace two years later. But the year 1962 must have been a particularly tragic one for the family, first in August when Thelma died from cancer aged just 29, and then in November when her father Sid died aged 60.

In 1930 Clara's other child from her first marriage, Rene, married Albert Henry Weaving, a gardener working at the nurseries in Langstone, a few miles east of Newport. Her grandmother, Clara's mother, Amelia Lucy Palmer was one of the witnesses at the ceremony at the local parish church. At some point Albert and Rene moved to Coventry, as with others almost certainly because the burgeoning motor car industry in the city provided far better job prospects than were available in South Wales. Indeed, in due course Albert was an electrician at the Rolls Royce company works. Rene was widowed in 1969, and she died in Coventry in 1983; the couple were very close, but had no children. A friend told me that when Rene was dying she was heard to call out the name of her brother Sid, who had died years earlier.

As to Clara and Mark's other children, Ernest Clifford and his wife Gladys adopted two daughters - Margaret and Carol. Edith Phyllis had four children - Sylvia, Brinley, William Geoffrey, and Stephen - while Gladys had four sons, Tony, David, Graham and Phillip.

18

Hard times

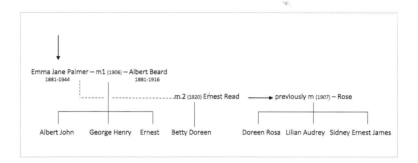

*E*mma Jane Palmer was born in 1881, the year which began in Cardiff with the worst blizzards ever to hit Wales. In 1906, when she was living at 134 Moorland Road Cardiff she married Albert Beard, a dock labourer from Bridgend Street, Cardiff who was born in Barnstaple in 1875. Soon after they married, Albert went to work at Guest, Keen & Nettlefolds iron and steel manufacturers as a boilerman. By 1910 they had rejoined Emma's family in Mill Road Ely, and in the summer of the year they had twin sons named George Henry and Albert John, known as Bert. In April 1915 Emma and Albert had another son who they named Ernest (picture 36).

In 1911 Albert had suffered a head injury in an accident at work, and soon after Ernest was born he was again injured at work, this time to the hand. For both of these injuries he received compensation, which might have eased the family's financial impact somewhat. But in May 1916 he developed an infected toe, and had to give up work for a while. He returned to work in July, but the infection resurfaced after just a week and Albert was admitted to hospital. While he was in hospital a toe operation failed to eradicate the infection, and the poor condition in which he was admitted gradually worsened. While modern-day treatment would be relatively straightforward by way of antibiotics, they did not exist at that time, and Albert died on 10 August 1916, aged just 42.

At the inquest, Emma gave evidence that Albert had told her that the infection was either caused by a protruding nail in his boot, or by a reaction to the boiler scales on which he worked. A witness told the Coroner that Albert had told him that the cause was the protruding nail. The Coroner held that the cause of Albert's death was septicemia brought on by the nail in his boot, and that he had contracted the infection fourteen weeks before he died. The Coroner made no reference to the boilers at work, and said that there was no evidence that any of Albert's earlier injuries had been a contributory cause, thus presumably removing any grounds for industrial compensation for his family. Albert was 42 years old, and the children were still very young, so Emma and the boys moved in with Emma's brother Edwin at 54 Mill Road.

It is worth noting what a tragic period this was for the family: Emma lost her 42-year-old husband and her 37-year-old sister Clara within the space of twelve weeks. Emma had two children aged six and one, and as we have seen Clara's own death led to the break-up of her branch of the family. And of course, most of her brothers were away on war service.

But with considerable help from the family Emma was able to keep her children together, and on 14 February 1920 at Conway Road Wesleyan Church, Cardiff, she married again, to her first cousin, a widower called Ernest James Read, who was three years her junior. The marriage was witnessed by Emma's brother William, and by Mabel Witts, her sister-in-law. Ernest was the son of Elizabeth Read, the unfortunate older sister of Emma's father, John Lush Palmer.

Ernest, a signalman with the Great Western Railway, had lived in Byron Street, Aberdare, with his first wife Rose, who he married in 1907 but who had died in childbirth, and their daughter Doreen Rosa who was born in

1909 but who died aged just three. Ernest and Rose had two more children: Lilian Audrey Read, (known as Audrey), born in Wilton in late 1911, and Sidney Ernest James Read (known as Sonny), born in Merthyr in 1914, just as his father was going to war.

Before he married Emma, Ernest had volunteered for war service: mandatory conscription didn't begin until 1916. Driver 33740 E. J. Read was one of the *'Old Contemptibles'* with the Royal Field Artillery (RFA) and fought at Mons, Britain's first battle of the war, on 23 August 1914. The RFA was equipped with the 18-pounder quick-firing field gun which, along with the smaller 13-pounder gun, was the mainstay of British field artillery for the rest of the war. The RFA also operated field batteries armed with the 4.5-inch howitzer. Ernest's job was to ride the gun limbers into and out of action: the gun limber consisted of a steel frame, two steel chests, wheels, axles and a draft connection for two or four horses or a tractor unit. The wheels were 60 inches in diameter with six-inch wide steel tyres, but no brakes. When carrying two shells, the limber weighed 2240 pounds (picture 37).

Ernest was awarded the 1914 Star, issued to all ranks who served in France or Belgium between 5 August 1914, the date of Britain's declaration of war against Germany and Austria-Hungary, and midnight on 22/23 November 1914, the end of the First Battle of Ypres. The medal was known as the Mons Star. He was also awarded the commemorative Victory Medal and British War Medal: together these three medals were known as 'Pip, Squeak and Wilfred'. Like the other members of the family who served, Ernest was fortunate to reach demob relatively unscathed, though he did lose three fingertips.

Emma Jane and her three Beard children moved to join the Reads in Aberdare when she married Ernest, who was always known as 'Pop' Read. Emma and Ernest had a daughter, Betty Doreen, born in June 1921. The family was then living at 2 Wenallt Road, Aberdare, where Ernest worked in the coal mines, as in due course did Emma's three sons (picture 38).

The Welsh valleys suffered badly in the Depression, and the family were helped out again by Emma's brother Edwin. Unemployment among coalminers rose from 2% in April 1924 to 12.5% in January 1925 and to 28.5% in August. The South Wales coalfield, more dependent upon exports than the other British coalfields, was the worst hit. In 1926 a major dispute across the coalfield led to a prolonged miners' strike, lock-out and much hardship between 1 May and 2 December. A countrywide general strike in support of the miners lasted barely a week before collapsing. Contrary to the miners' hopes, the outcome of this bitter confrontation was the widespread blacklisting of strikers, a 20% reduction in wages and the imposition of an eight-hour day on those workers who were able to return to work. The three Beard boys left school when they were barely into their teens, taking on a number of jobs in order to keep the family's head above water.

But in the 1930s a prolonged economic depression ensued and blighted the lives of a generation across the South Wales coalfield, linked as it was to a contraction of the coal industry and the crisis in international finance following the Wall Street Crash of 1929. The decade was a time of mass unemployment and of continuous and heavy migration from the Cynon Valley and similar mining communities. So it was that in the mid-1930s Ernest and George Beard moved to Coventry, where there were secure and well-paid jobs in the motor industry, and as I've related earlier their cousins, Albert and Leonard Pittard, were also there in the 1930s. But by the start of World War II the Reads and the Beards had moved to Langstone to join Emma's parents. 'Pop' Read was then working as a carpenter.

Emma's stepson Sonny, a bricklayer, was married to Elsie and they lived in Whitchurch, Cardiff. In 1939, when war against Germany was inevitable, Sonny was one of an army of bricklayers employed by a Cardiff company to construct an enormous munitions filling factory at Glascoed, near Pontypool. Building work on the 1,000-acre site, which would eventually comprise over 700 separate buildings, had started in February 1938. The factory was officially opened in April 1940, but in that same month

The building of the hospital was completed in February 1915 (picture 49), though by that time Albert and Alfred had moved back to Minnesota. It seems probable that they set up home there: Albert certainly was still there in 1917, living above a metal-plating company at 408 Second Avenue East, just 200 metres from the Mississippi river, although by then Alfred had returned to Wales, summoned by another brother to join the fight against the German forces in northern France.

Neither the hospital nor Forest City itself survived nearly as long as the two brothers. The hospital was dismantled some years later, and about thirty-five years after their visit much of the town was deliberately flooded when a series of dams was constructed along the Missouri.

Eventually the war in Europe called Albert as well, albeit by a different route. On 10 October 1917 in Winnipeg he joined the Canadian Overseas Expeditionary Force (picture 50). Happily, Albert's wartime records were safely stored far away from Hitler's bombs, in Canada, so I am at least able to share some detail about his service. He was paid $1·10 a day, and he requested that $20 a month from his pay should be sent direct to his mother. It seems he did not encounter action, and this is almost certainly explained in his medical report which noted that since childhood he had suffered from poor eyesight, and although he was deemed fit for service abroad he was not able to get into the infantry. In January 1918 he was assigned to the Canadian Army Service Corps and in due course was posted to the UK, where he landed on 4 March 1918 (picture 51).

He spent about three months at Dibgate Camp, Shorncliffe, neat Hythe in Kent, from where the sounds of the big guns across the channel could often be heard. In June 1918 he was posted to Seaford with the 18th Reserve Battalion. Seaford Camp in Sussex was a Canadian training facility that provided accommodation for reserves and served as the headquarters of the Canadian Engineers Training Centre and the Canadian Machine Gun Depot. In July 1918 Albert was transferred to the Canadian Forestry Corps, based at Sunningdale in Berkshire, although shortly afterwards he was posted to Inverness. The Forestry Corps was created when it was discovered that huge quantities of wood were needed for use on the Western Front. Duckboards, shoring timbers, crates – anything that needed wood had to be provided. The British government concluded that there was nobody more experienced or qualified in the British Empire to harvest timber than the Canadians.

In June 1918, shortly before he was demobbed, he married Florence Nicholls, with permission from his Commanding Officer (picture 52). Albert had known Florence since before the war, and had sent her a postcard on the day he left Liverpool for the United States in 1913 (pictures 53 and 54). Following the Armistice in November 1918, Albert was granted leave over the Christmas season, returning to Inverness in January 1919. In March he was posted back to Sunningdale, and soon afterwards was transferred to the Canadian camp in Rhyl, North Wales, from where he was discharged, his papers being marked *'service no longer required'*. Albert returned home to Ely, where he and Florence had a son, Arthur Henry Palmer.

But by 1924 Albert had followed his parents to Langstone, where he lived in a house called *Hiawatha*, no doubt named as a consequence of his travels in America; in fact he would later live in a house called *Dakota*. Together with his brother Alfred, Albert built the Wesleyan Methodist Church in Langstone, and his mother Amelia laid the foundation stone that bears her name (pictures 55 to 58). He also built an identical chapel at Rogiet, in the same county. Albert also built the houses which formed Catsash Road in Langstone, which at that time formed most of the village to the north of the main Cardiff-to-London road.

Albert and several of his brothers were members of what was then known as the Grand Lodge of the Loyal Order of Moose. The Order came to the UK in 1926 when its founder in the USA established the UK arm of the Grand Lodge in South Wales at his birthplace in Tredegar. The organisation, which is now multi-national, raises funds for many charities, though at the time that the Palmer brothers were members it was specifically directed towards helping the orphaned and the widowed. In the 1930s Albert was organist in the Order's Progress Lodge in Newport, despite a souvenir book commemorating the visit of the King and Queen to Newport in 1937 describing him as the Lodge's *'organiser'* – it might have been a misprint, though I've no doubt he could have done both jobs!

Florence died in 1951, and the following year Albert married Phyllis Stent, a dental nurse from Newport, who was twenty years his junior. In due course they lived at Tidenham near Chepstow, in a house with a spectacular view overlooking a horseshoe bend in the River Wye, a property which British TV personality Alan Whicker once tried unsuccessfully to buy.

Albert died in September 1964, survived by Phyllis who died in 1999 leaving the bulk of her estate to a donkey sanctuary in Devon. Arthur died in May 2007, leaving four children, twins Felicity Ann and Faith Elizabeth, and sons Stephen and James.

20

Minding the business

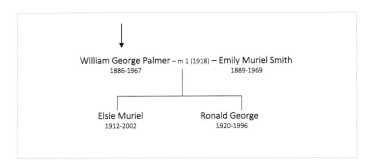

William George Palmer – m 1 (1918) – Emily Muriel Smith
1886-1967   1889-1969

Elsie Muriel   Ronald George
1912-2002   1920-1996

*W*illiam George Palmer was born in 1886. When he was a teenager William was working with his father in the brickworks as an errand boy. In August 1911 he married 22-year-old Emily Muriel Smith. The wedding was at Ely Methodist Church, to which as we have seen the family had very strong ties, in the new building that had been completed just three months earlier (picture 59).

In their native Gloucestershire, Emily's father Charles William Smith had been a hay trusser. But in the years before the marriage Emily was a housemaid to Dr. Charles Tanfield Vachell at 11 Park Place, in the centre of Cardiff. The photograph of 11 Park Place was actually a postcard written by Emily and sent to a friend (picture 60).

The Vachell family was one of Cardiff's best known. Dr. Vachell's father had made a fortune as an apothecary and druggist, played a key role in the implementation of the 1848 Public Health Act in Cardiff, and was twice Lord Mayor. His son and Emily's employer, Charles Tanfield Vachell, was a physician (picture 61). But he was also a naturalist who, working with his daughter Eleanor (who also lived at 11 Park Place and who became equally well-known in the field of botany) produced celebrated works on the flora of Wales, published early in the twentieth century. Dr. Vachell was instrumental in the foundation of the National Museum of Wales and played a leading role in the creation of a botanic garden in Cardiff's Roath Park. When practising as a physician he was probably based at the nearby Cardiff Royal Infirmary.

After their marriage William and Emily lived at 26 Mill Road. They had two children, Elsie Muriel born in August 1912, and Ronald George born in July 1920. In 1916 William and Emily were living at 5 Kingsland Road, a few streets east of Victoria Park. William was the only one of John Lush Palmer's sons who did not serve in World War I: this was because he was working on the land and managing the business. In 1921, William and Emily were living with Albert at 35 Cowbridge Road, and William and Emily were still there through the 1930s after which they moved along the road to a larger house at number 59 (picture 62).

William managed the Windsor Gardens nurseries for many years, until his son Ronald took over. Throughout, the nurseries retained the name of 'J Palmer and Sons' (picture 63). In later years, William and Emily lived in Thompson Avenue, a few minutes' walk from Victoria Park Bowls Club, where William and some of his brothers were members and regular players. William and Emily both died in St. David's, Pembrokeshire, William in 1967 and Emily in 1979 (picture 64).

21

The grieving mother

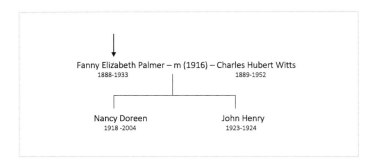

Fanny Elizabeth Palmer – m (1916) – Charles Hubert Witts
1888-1933   1889-1952

Nancy Doreen   John Henry
1918 -2004   1923-1924

*F*anny Elizabeth Palmer was born in 1888. On 14 October 1916 she married Charles Hubert Witts (picture 65). Charlie, as he was known, had lived with his father George a gardener, mother Eliza a laundress, and younger sister Mabel Louise, who at the age of seventeen was a music teacher and who ten years later would marry Fanny's brother Alfred (picture 66).

The Witts family hailed from Gloucestershire, but had moved to South Wales in the early 1890s, eventually living in Ely at 32 Riverside Terrace, close to the Palmers' Windsor Nurseries, and to the new homes that the Palmers were occupying nearby in Mill Road. Charlie had been an insurance agent, but in 1911 a train driver called John Lewis was boarding with the Witts family, which quite possibly led to Charlie obtaining work with Great Western Railway, initially as a porter earning eighteen shillings a week, and then as a goods checker at Cardiff Goods Station. Charlie also served in the Great War (picture 67).

After they married, Fanny and Charlie set up home in Mill Road. On

25 July 1918, they had a daughter, Nancy Doreen (picture 68), who later attended Lansdowne Road School, and a son John Henry born on 26 September 1923. By the following year, Charlie was working as a railway shunter when tragedy struck on Boxing Day at 56 Mill Road as baby John died from pneumonia. He was 15 months old (picture 69).

Fanny grieved for John for many years, and she died in 1933 from tuberculosis after a long illness. Fifteen-year-old Nancy had to keep house and look after her father, a task at which, according to letters written in the 1940s by several of her uncles, she excelled. In 1942, Nancy married Cyril James, and eventually they came to live next door to Emma Jane and her family in Langstone, where Nancy worked as a lunch lady at the local primary school. In 1945 Charlie remarried, to a widow named Elsie Cappellan, whose husband had died the previous year.

Nancy's father Charlie Witts died in 1952, aged 63.

32. The family and a potato crop. William Palmer is on the left wearing the hat. Emma Jane Beard is on the right with her young son Ernest. The others are probably members of the Pittard and Jones familes.

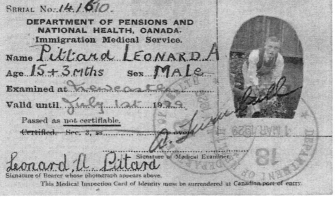

33. Leonard Pittard's immigration medical card, March 1929.

34. Leonard Pittard's letter to National Children's Homes HQ, 1929.

Dear Sir

I am writing to ask you if I will be able able to go to Canada with the August party, to join my younger brother. I have been able to learn many other things since March in the garden under the direction of Mr Hodgson our gardener. I can now do good work with the spade, and will do my best if I get the chance to go to Canada, and I want want to be earning my own living. Trusting you can help me in this matter

Yours Truly,
Leonard Pittard.

35. National Children's Home inspection record re Albert Pittard, 1933.

36. Emma Jane Beard with (l-r) George, Albert & Ernest, approx 1916.

37. Ernest James Read (second from right) loading the gun, World War 1.

38. Ernest James Read and Emma with their families, probably late-1930s. L to r: Back: George Beard, Ernest Beard, 'Sonny' Read, Albert Beard. Centre: Lilian Audrey Read, Ernest James Read, Emma Jane Read. Front: Betty Read.

39. 'Sonny' Read, 1940.

40. Albert Palmer, bricklayer, approx 1905.

41. Albert Palmer.

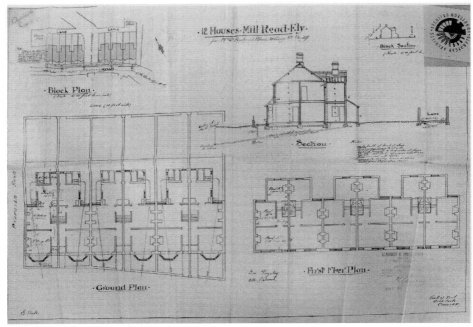

42. Albert Palmer's plans for new houses in Mill Road, Ely, 1907.

43. Children outside houses built by Albert Palmer in Mill Road, Ely. They probably include Palmer children.

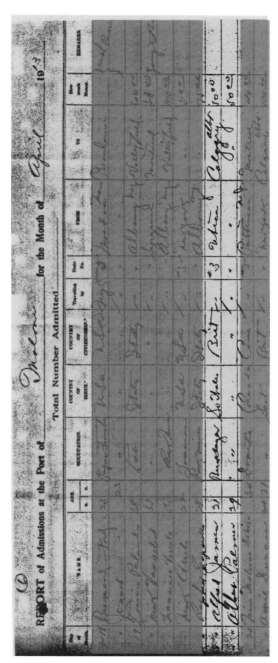

44. Immigration record from USA into Canada, Albert & Alfred Palmer, April 1913.

45. Calgary Cyclone, 1912.

46. Immigration record from Canada into USA, Albert & Alfred Palmer, September 1914.

47. Construction of Bagley High School.

48. Forest City Press article, 7 October 1914.

49. Construction of Forest City Cheyenne Agency Hospital.

50. Albert Palmer in Canadian Army uniform, World War 1.

51. Albert Palmer outside the 'rat hut', World War 1.

52. Florence Palmer, nee Nicholls.

53. Postcard sent by Albert Palmer to Florence Nicholls, 1913.

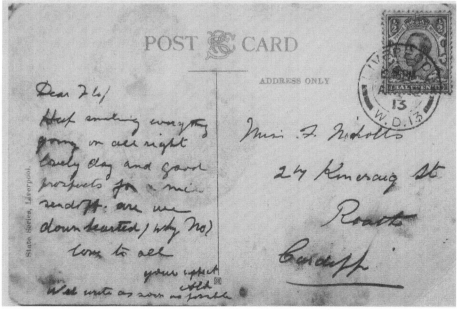

54. Message on back of postcard.

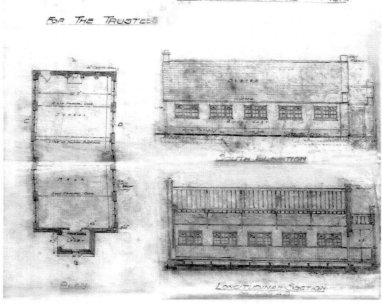

55. Plans for Wesleyan Methodist Church, Langstone.

56. Laying of foundation stone, Langstone Methodist Church. Amelia
Lucy Palmer is on far left

57. Construction of Langstone Methodist Church.

58. Langstone Methodist Church 2014.

59. William & Emily Palmer's wedding, 1911. Identified are l-r: back row: 3 Florence Nicholls, 5 Charles Witts, 6 Fanny Witts, 7 Alfred Palmer. Middle row: 2 Mark Pittard, 4 Emily, 5 William, 6 Amelia Lucy Palmer, 7 John Lush Palmer, 8 Walter Palmer. Front: 1 Clara Pittard with babies Edith Phyllis and Ernest Clfford, 2 Herbert Palmer, 5 Nellie Palmer, 6 Ethel Irene Jones, 8 Sidney Jones, 9 Emma Jane Beard with twin babies George and Albert. It is likely that the man with the white beard is John Palmer, John Lush Palmer's father, but this cannot be confirmed.

60. The Vachell home in Park Place, Cardiff, appoximately 1911.

61. Charles Tansfield Vachell.

62. William Palmer (right) with his brother Albert.

63. William Palmer leading the company horse. His younger brother Walter is riding on the cart.

64. Four generations: William, Elsie and Amelia Lucy Palmer, with Elsie's baby daughter Muriel, approx 1937.

22

Heroes and villains

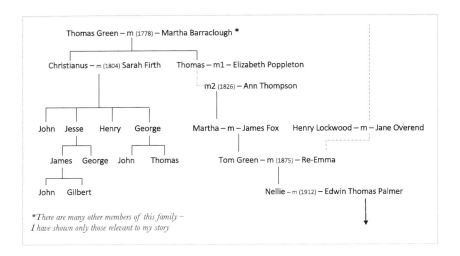

Thomas Green – m (1778) – Martha Barraclough *

Christianus – m (1804) Sarah Firth   Thomas – m1 – Elizabeth Poppleton

m2 (1826) – Ann Thompson

John   Jesse   Henry   George   Martha – m – James Fox   Henry Lockwood – m – Jane Overend

James   George   John   Thomas   Tom Green – m (1875) – Re-Emma

John   Gilbert   Nellie – m (1912) – Edwin Thomas Palmer

*There are many other members of this family –
I have shown only those relevant to my story*

I must pause for a while before I move on to John and Amelia's next child, Edwin. This story has so far focused on the Palmer line, and the direct ancestors I have described have all been called Palmer or married a Palmer. But with the reader's forbearance I will now jump back over a century, and move for a short while to the other side of the family tree – and also to the other side of the Atlantic Ocean, via Yorkshire – before bringing the story back to the Palmers in South Wales. A man called Thomas Green was born in Doncaster in 1757, and he was my great-great-great-great-grandfather on my paternal grandmother's side.

In 1778 Thomas married Martha Barraclough at Campsall Parish Church near Doncaster. The first part of their married life was spent at Norton, but they moved to Horbury sometime before December 1796.

Thomas, a carpenter by trade and a Wesleyan Methodist, and Martha produced at least twelve children: several died young, notably in one tragic spell in the winter of 1804-05 when four of them died in less than three months. However, I will concentrate on just two of the survivors, Christianus Green and Thomas Green.

My great-great-great-great-uncle Christianus Green was christened on Christmas Day 1780, which might explain his unusual forename. Christianus himself is not part of the direct line, but a summary of his own family story illustrates the breadth and variety of the wider family. Christianus spent most of his life in Yorkshire, and married Sarah Firth in 1804. Over the next seventeen years they produced seven children, all born and raised in Horbury. But in the early 1840s two of his sons, John and Jesse, emigrated to the USA and in 1844, by which time their youngest child was aged 22, Christianus and Sarah, by then in their mid-sixties, followed them to the USA and settled in Wisconsin. A third son, Henry, followed them later.

Christianus was a man of moral and intellectual worth, and a highly respected member of the community. Many years later he was described thus in the *Wesleyan Recorder*:

> *A local worthy of middle height, well-built frame, florid complexion, quick eye and close cropped hair, he was a man to arrest attention; and wearing, as he did on Sundays, kerseymere knee breeches and leggings, a white handkerchief, and broad-brimmed hat, he presented a striking and picturesque appearance. And his character corresponded; he was a man of mark and individuality, having an extensive acquaintance with men and things, and being able to speak well on most subjects, he was ever welcome in public and private, and for miles around his discourses were listened to with intense delight. In politics he was a liberal. A loyal subject, he nevertheless sympathised with those who were seeking reform both in Church and State.*

The three sons of Christianus who moved to America, and their offspring, successfully lived the American Dream. The eldest, John, became a wool-weaver and farmer in Missouri, although sadly when he died in 1856, aged 48 and just a month before his own father Christanus died, he left six children aged between three and thirteen; they seem to have done well nevertheless: one became a lawyer and a banker, and another a physician.

Christianus's next son Jesse worked for a time in mining, and by 1850 he was mining in El Dorado, California and lodging with a group of Welshmen. His presence there at that time is unsurprising: on a cold morning early in 1848, a carpenter from New Jersey had picked up a few nuggets of gold from the American river, and the Great Gold Rush had begun. Later Jesse bought a farm and spent the rest of his life in agriculture, until he received a fatal injury in a fall.

Finally Cristianus's son Henry, '*a man of rare mental power and great loveliness of character*', served as County Supervisor in Jo Daviess *(sic)* County, before being elected to the State Legislature. He served three terms, and then was elected State Senator for two terms.

Jesse's son James, one of twelve, was successful in many different lines of business and acquired enough wealth to enable him to live in comfort. He was a Justice of the Peace, spent six years as superintendent of a large farm, then '*engaged in the mercantile business, selling out in less than a year*', which enabled him to buy a farm where he lived for 24 years, during which time he also had interests in grain, coal and lumber. In 1900, another of Jesse's sons, George Green, described his occupation in the Jo Daviess County census form as '*capitalist*', so one presumes he did well for himself.

In turn, James's own sons John and Gilbert also did well. John was a scientist – a magnetician. He undertook geological surveys in many parts of the world, and developed standards used by the world's leading centres of excellence in the field, including the Carnegie Institute and the Magnetic Observatory in Washington DC. In World War II he was engaged in defence work at the Carnegie Institute and worked for the US Office of Scientific Research. John retired to Fort Lauderdale, Florida. Gilbert graduated from Dental College with distinguished honours following a mark of 99%, the highest ever awarded. His college offered him a professorship, which he declined, preferring to take up a practice himself. Having practised dentistry for 30 years, he moved to California where he acquired interests in real estate and insurance, and obtained a realtor's licence. He also was connected to a company engaged in drilling and oil exploration.

The offspring of Christianus and Sarah's other children who remained in Horbury also deserve a mention. John, son of George, was educated at private schools in Leeds and Wakefield. He was director and one-time managing partner of Hartley Green & Co, woollen manufacturers, and was for many years honorary secretary of the Leeds Philharmonic. He *'combined an artistic temperament with a grip on practical methods'*, was praised for the way he arranged and managed the orchestra's foreign tours, and was an enthusiastic member of the Badsworth Hunt in Yorkshire. John's brother Thomas undertook experimental work in photography, and apparently he famously refused to sell an invention to Pathé; regrettably I have not been able to discover what it was.

Christianus lived in his adopted land for thirteen years, *'ever zealous for the best interests of the people, and died in 1856, a true Christian and an honest Radical reformer'*. Together with about a dozen of his very large family, he is buried in a cemetery plot in Weston, Illinois.

But if Christianus and his offspring led virtuous and successful lives on both sides of the Atlantic, it's fair to say that his brother Thomas junior led a rather different one, and seemingly moved in very different circles. Thomas junior was my great-great-great-grandfather on my paternal grandmother's side.

Thomas lived in Horbury, and was a carpenter. When he was 31 years old, he became implicated in the Luddite upheavals which rocked the West Riding of Yorkshire in 1812. The term Luddite is often used today to refer to anybody who is stubbornly opposed to new technology; but Luddism was a protest movement of the early 1800s and was much more than a crude attempt to 'uninvent' new machinery. The Luddites were in reality skilled textile workers who protested against the use of new labour-replacing machinery between 1811 and 1817. The stocking frames, spinning frames and power looms introduced during the Industrial Revolution threatened to replace them with less-skilled, low-wage labourers, leaving them without work. Many crimes were committed, either directly concerned with the wrecking of machinery or indirectly through the theft of money, tools and arms with which to mount their campaign of violence and damage. The act of breaking machines could lead to death on the gallows, so unsurprisingly secrecy was paramount. Throughout 1812 there were numerous attacks in and around Huddersfield. In an attempt to hide their tracks, the Luddites carried out their crimes in the name of *'Ned Ludd'* their semi-mythical leader, who was reputed to be one George Mellor, from Longroyd Bridge, near Huddersfield.

Thomas Green was accused of being part of a gang that *'feloniously and burglariously'* broke into the house, near Netherton, of one Abraham Moore and carried off various articles. On 17 September 1812, he was arrested and committed to the gaol in York Castle. A report to the Home Secretary on the same date reads:

> *I have the honour to acquaint your Lordship by order of Mr. Ratcliffe our Magistrate that he has this Morning committed Thomas Green to York Castle for Burglary on the Information of Earl Parkin, a Copy of whose Examination I had the honour to send to your Lordship yesterday, and I beg to observe that we can confirm Parkin's Evidence out of the Mouth of two other Witnesses.*

On the same day Stockport solicitor John Lloyd also wrote to the Home Office, saying:

> *One of the Gang, Thomas Green, has been this day committed by Mr. Radcliffe to York upon the Evidence of Parkin whom we will get supported by corroborative circumstances. The commitment is for a Burglary on Abraham*

112

Moor whom I yesterday examined, but I shall be able to prove him one of those that have stolen arms at other places ...

Also in the gaol was the aforementioned George Mellor, and on 30 November in a letter smuggled out of the gaol he asked that Thomas Green's name be added to a petition seeking a more peaceful attempt at reform, through Parliament. This was almost certainly a pre-trial attempt by Mellor to be seen more as a political campaigner than a criminal.

The trial, by a Special Commission from the Home Secretary, opened at York on 2 January 1813. The only evidence against Thomas Green had come from Parkin, who had turned King's Evidence in an attempt to escape trial himself. But Parkin's evidence had not been corroborated, and the prosecutor, James Park, conceded that Thomas Green and some others had been under the influence and control of defendants who had already been convicted. No Bill of Indictment was proffered against Green and he was discharged, although the Prosecutor added the caveat that '*my forbearance, at present, does not exempt them from enquiry at a future time if their conduct should not entitle them to that forbearance*'. An intriguing possibility was raised in '*The Risings of The Luddites*' (1880) by Frank Peel, in which the author refers to Green *et al* being discharged because he himself was an informer, though there seems no firm evidence to support this claim. After a ten-day trial, and as Green undoubtedly breathed a sigh of relief, other defendants were convicted, largely on the evidence of the informers Earl Parkin and his brother Samuel. Many were ordered to be transported, but death sentences were pronounced on fourteen others; they were duly hanged at York Castle on 16 January 1813.

The reader will have already noted that some twenty years later the farming Palmers in Wiltshire were to encounter, and perhaps be involved in, similar violent protests directed towards threshing machines, and riots that led to death sentences and transportations.

Thomas Green's first wife Elizabeth died in 1826. Later that year he remarried, to Ann Thompson, and four years later they had a daughter called Martha, who became a tailoress in Horbury. In 1852, Martha married a Huddersfield mechanic called James Fox. They in turn had a son named Tom Green Fox; he was born in Huddersfield in 1854, and in 1875 he married a wool weaver from Huddersfield named Re-Emma Lockwood.

Re-Emma's father Henry Lockwood (a pit deputy in a coalmine) had died in suspicious circumstances: in March 1889 he was found dead in the River Calder near Dewsbury with two deep head wounds, which had caused his death rather than drowning. His friends were nearby, heard him fall into the water, and extracted him quite quickly. Although the Coroner accepted the inquest jury's verdict of accidental death, it is clear from the report of the inquest that he had doubts about the circumstances of how Henry's body got into the river. Certainly, in later years Henry's granddaughter maintained that he had been deliberately killed, though as she was not quite two years old at the time of the incident it seems likely that she was perpetuating a belief that had come from her parents, rather than giving contemporaneous evidence.

That granddaughter's name was Nellie, and in 1891 when she was four she moved to Cardiff with her parents. Nellie's mother died in 1900. Nellie and her father, who remarried in 1901, lived at 110 Glenroy Street in Roath, a district of Cardiff that borders onto Splott where the Palmers were living. Nellie attended Albany Road School, and then found work as a shop assistant around the same time that my grandfather, Edwin Thomas Palmer, was apprenticed to a grocer called Mr Pugh, who had two shops in the neighbourhood, one in Meteor Street, and one in City Road (picture 70). The happy coincidence of a juxtaposition of grocery shops, and of Edwin and Nellie working in close proximity, allows me to return to the Palmer line.

23

The entrepreneur

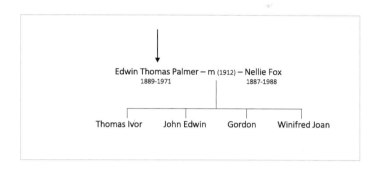

Edwin Thomas Palmer – m (1912) – Nellie Fox
1889-1971   1887-1988

Thomas Ivor   John Edwin   Gordon   Winifred Joan

*E*dwin Thomas Palmer, always known as Ted, was born in 1889. It was soon clear that Ted was not going to follow his father into the world of market gardening, and he set his sights on the retail business. To learn the trade, Ted was an apprentice at Pugh's grocery store in City Road, in the Roath district of Cardiff, where he lodged at the shop with some other apprentice boys. In due course Ted met Nellie at Pugh's, a five-minute walk from her home.

Nellie's introduction to the Palmer family was most memorable for her enormous hat, which - as later described by Ted's brother Herbert - had '*the garden of Eden on the top*', and for the remarks of Ted's elder brothers, describing her as '*a swell bit*', '*a nice bit of stuff*', and '*a Bobby Dazzler*' (picture 71). She was also said to have displayed some bravado by riding an old horse called White Charlie a mile or two out in the country to Woodlands, the new home of former Mill Road neighbours the Thomases, for a wager.

In 1911 when he was a 22-year-old grocer's assistant, Ted was boarding in Mill Road with his sister Emma Jane and her husband and young twins, and was working with a grocer in Mill Road. In 1912 Ted married Nellie at Ely Methodist Church, with Ted's brother Alfred as his Best Man. Ted and Nellie had their first child, Thomas Ivor (Tom, my father) in May 1913 and a second, John Edwin (always known as Jack) in May 1914 (picture 72).

Christmas parties were always special occasions in Ted's household: I remember them well from the 1950s, but they were happening as long ago as 1914 at 54 Mill Road, where Ted and Nellie were living next door to Emma Jane and Albert. But that year's party was almost a tragic occasion, when the Father Christmas beard and costume worn by Ted caught fire as he reached over some decorative candles. One of the children present later recalled that she had wanted to stay in the room because she thought it was Father Christmas's way of going back up the chimney, but fortunately Ted's young brothers Walter and Herbert knew better and stripped him of his clothes and doused the flames. Ted was quite badly burned, though in later years the incident, perhaps understandably, became something of a family joke (picture 73).

But that year brought darker times, and like so many others Ted volunteered for service at the start of the Great War, probably in the Army Service Corps. I know little about Ted's service, although his younger brother Alfred, whom I shall discuss shortly, later recalled an emotional meeting with Ted on the Somme in 1916, so we do know he was there (picture 74). He was also at the Battle of Passchendaele, fought between July and November 1917 for control of the ridges south and east of the Belgian city of Ypres in West Flanders, close to the railway junction at Roeselare, which was a vital part of the supply system of the German Fourth Army. The battle ended in November when the Canadian Corps captured Passchendaele. Fought in appalling weather conditions, the campaign was and still is controversial and - although the figures are often disputed - British casualties (killed and injured) were around a quarter of a million, while German casualties were perhaps double that figure.

While Ted was away at war Nellie, when not looking after their baby boys and helping out the wider family, used to knit socks to send out to the troops. Sometimes Ted and Nellie's lifelong family friends Trevor and Gwladys Chichester helped to care for the babies at their home in Wellfield Terrace. Ted sent postcards from the front to each of his children. One card to Tom (picture 75) is embroidered on the front with the words '*I'm thinking of you*', and the message on the reverse reads '*April 22nd 1917: To Dear Tommy, with love from Daddy*'. The card would have been written as the British forces and their allies were fighting around the French town of Arras.

When the war was over Ted and Nellie, still living at 54 Mill Road, had two more children, Gordon born 1918, and Winifred Joan (Winnie) born 1923. Many years later Ted joked that he only had four children because after Winnie was born he found out the cause! Ted resumed his job as a grocer, and in about 1923 he bought a shop near the family homes in Mill Road and started his own grocery business. In 1927 the business was threatened when the shop and its contents were severely damaged as storms caused the River Ely to flood again and severe gales blew the roofs off houses in Cowbridge Road. But with help – including that from some of Ted's competitors – the business recovered. By 1928 he had a second shop in Cowbridge Road East, about a mile from Mill Road, and at the same time obtained planning permission to extend the Mill Road shop. The Cowbridge Road business was at number 494 (near Victoria Park), though it soon moved along to 508 Cowbridge Road.

So Ted had become a successful businessman, and for a while he owned a Dunelt motorcycle (picture 76 – advertised as '*the machine with the supercharged engine*') with a sidecar into which the four children would often be squeezed for trips to the seaside – once with unfortunate consequences as the bike and its contents veered off the road into a ditch on the Tumble Hill to the west of Cardiff; luckily nobody was badly hurt. Soon Ted was one of the few people in the area to own a car in the 1920s, a Morris Cowley, which afforded rather more comfortable – and much safer – transport for family outings.

Business success meant that Ted and Nellie became financially comfortable; but they were generous to members of the family and friends who encountered hard times. During the Depression in the late-1920s they took food on a weekly basis to Emma Jane's family in Aberdare. They took hot soup and supplies to families who were marooned by floods, and they visited friends and family who were ill or going through hard times, often leaving cash or provisions hidden in the house until they had left. In 1929 they left Mill Road, having bought a house at 29 Victoria Park Road West. In the same year, Ted became a Freemason, and was enrolled into the Gwalia Lodge in Cardiff (picture 77). He remained a member of the Lodge for thirty years, during which time he was involved in charity fundraising. He also worked with the Cardiff-based charity Tenovus, now a major charity in the field of cancer research and support provision, but in Ted's time a relatively small local charity which raised funds for a wide range of activities.

In February 1933 the Cardiff Public Works Committee approved Ted's plans to erect three shops, two flats and five lock-up garages (picture 78). The building was completed remarkably quickly, and the shops opened in September 1933. The building at 514 Cowbridge Road, on the corner of Mayfield Avenue, was completed by Blacker & Sons, builders. Two of the shops were occupied by Ted as grocery and greengrocery businesses, while the third was a butcher's shop. The total cost was £2,832, which was paid by stage payments while the building was under way. Palmer's Stores, 514 Cowbridge Road East, was to be the family business centre for over forty years until the property was sold to Lloyds Bank (pictures 79 and 80). All three of Ted's sons worked in the Cowbridge Road shop, Tom and Jack for the whole of their working lives and Gordon for much of his.

Ted was an official of the Cardiff and District Grocers' Association. In 1934 he was its president, and during the ensuing war years he was treasurer and representative on the Council of the Federation of Grocers' Associations of the United Kingdom, where he was often involved in discussions on the vexed question of maintaining food supplies during wartime (picture 81). In later years he was appointed president of the National Federation, which brought him into contact with some of the most important people in the world of food and provisions supply (picture 82). There is no doubt that his commercial success was in no small part the result of his leadership in the grocery trade and his ability to draw on contacts, especially in the Second World War when he seemed able to obtain commodities unavailable to others.

My father Tom married Vesta Mary Matthews, always known as Cissie, in 1939 (picture 83). Jack also married in 1939, to Doris Pugh. The other children waited until after the war: Winnie married Eric Treseder in 1945, bringing together Cardiff's two horticultural dynasties, Winnie being the granddaughter of John Lush Palmer, and Eric being the grandson of horticulturalist Fred Treseder, renowned as the creator of the 'Bishop of Llandaff' dahlia which he cultivated in the 1920s and which became one of Britain's most popular flowers. Lastly Gordon married Eileen Hardy in 1949. My parents, Tom and Cissie, had two children, Brian born in 1940 and me, born in 1946.

Ted and Nellie continued to enjoy the fruits of success, and during the 1950s, when most Cardiffians took a seaside holiday if they could afford one in resorts such as Tenby and Torquay, they travelled regularly to Cannes and Monte Carlo (picture 84), Switzerland and Italy, cruised in the Bahamas, and in 1959 crossed the Atlantic on the *RMS Queen Elizabeth* to tour the USA and Canada with their American friends and hosts Colonel and Mrs Richards. But they also enjoyed frequent trips to London, the south coast, and Scotland.

Ted saw himself very much as the patriarch overseeing his own large branch of the Palmer family, once comparing himself with the stag in Landseer's painting '*The Monarch of the Glen*'. He and Nellie much enjoyed gatherings of as many of the family as possible, on day trips to Porthcawl in the summer and Tintern Abbey in the autumn, and at their home at

Christmas when family and many friends would gather for food, music, games, and of course present-giving over which Ted presided – but thankfully without burning beards! Ted was of course astute and intelligent, but also sociable and possessed of a keen sense of humour. But it has to be said that there was another side to the patriarch. In Roman times the *pater familias* was not only the eldest male in the family: he also had complete control of the family members, who were expected to adhere to core principles he laid down. In Ted's case his 'rule' might not have been so overt, yet there were clear similarities. He allowed little space for his three sons to spread their wings, and for the most part they complied, meeting resentment on the rare occasions when they exercised, or tried to exercise, their own life decisions. The upshot was, as I have said, that his three sons spent most or all of their working lives in the family shop, to their own inevitable frustration and, often in a more outspoken way, that of their wives. It was perhaps significant that notwithstanding that the sons were directors, the shop sign always read Palmer's: no doubt the position of the apostrophe was deliberate.

Ted died at his home, 29 Victoria Park Road West, Cardiff, on 20 November 1971. Ted's Will, executed seven months before he died, shows that he then owned properties at 488 Cowbridge Road East; 510 and 512 Cowbridge Road East; 514 Cowbridge Road East (Palmer's Stores), 2B Mayfield Avenue; 29 Victoria Park Road West (his home); and 66 Mill Road. Nellie reached the age of 100 in August 1987, the occasion of perhaps the last major family party (pictures 85 and 86).

Nellie died five months later, in her 101st year. Ted and Nellie's son Jack died in August 1987, Gordon in April 1999, and Tom in February 2007, while their daughter Winnie died in September 2014.

24

Staunch to the end against odds uncounted

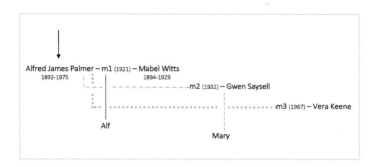

*A*lfred James Palmer was born in 1892. As a child, Alf used to wear his brother Ted's 'hand-me-down' clothes, and Ted used to read Charles Dickens' books to him at bedtime.

Like his older brother Albert, Alf was a bricklayer. In 1913, as I have already mentioned, the two of them set off on the perilous journey to America, with the intention of travelling to Canada to find work.

It seems that Alf's decision to accompany Albert to Canada was something of a last-minute one: at a meeting in late March 1913, the Sunday School Committee at his church recorded in its minutes

> *...now that Mr Alf Palmer was also emigrating to Canada with his brother*
> *...' and resolved that '... some kind of recognition should be made to him*
> *for the services he has rendered to the school so faithfully and that we regret to*
> *hear he is leaving us which will be a great loss to our school, but we hope and*
> *trust he will be of greater service to the Master in the other land.*

The Committee refused to accept Alf's resignation in the hope that he would return to teaching at the church at some future time. However, it is interesting that the word *'emigrating'* was used, suggesting that the two brothers intended their departure to be permanent. In my next chapter I recount many of the entries of Alf's diary of their journey.

I was told by his niece that Alf had volunteered for army service at the start of the Great War on his return from Canada, and that he served for the full four years of the war. I have an issue with that, because shipping records show that on the 22 January 1916 he sailed into Liverpool on board the White Star Line passenger ship *Adriatic* from New York City. The ship's manifest shows his occupation as bricklayer. Curiously, although his address is shown as 35 Windsor Terrace, Ely, his *'country of last permanent residence'* is recorded as USA. It also showed USA to be his country of *'intended future permanent residence'*, which is consistent with the reference in the Sunday School Committee minutes to his impending emigration. It is of course just feasible that he made this voyage while he was on active military service, but it seems improbable, especially taking into account the records to which I have just referred. Furthermore, the Military Service Act of 1916 which introduced mandatory conscription was passed in January and took effect in March, so this is almost certainly what brought Alf back home together with a summons from his brother: he wrote many years later that his brother Ted had called him *'from the deep south and brought me home to waste my time and the country's money in the blood and filth of Flanders.'* Quite what Albert meant by *'the deep south'* is a mystery, and I have no evidence that he ventured further south than New York City.

He started duty with the Royal Engineers, and in 1916 his base was a training camp at Coed Helen near Caernarfon in North Wales, where between 2,000 and 2,500 soldiers were accommodated in tents. Alf's uniform in later photographs suggest that he might at some time have transferred to the Army Service Corps (pictures 87 and 88).

What I can say for certain is that Alf, like Ted, saw action at the Battle of the Somme. Intended to be a decisive breakthrough, the Battle of the

Somme instead became a byword for futile and indiscriminate slaughter. Allied artillery pounded German lines for a week before the attack, firing 1.6 million shells. British commanders were so confident they ordered their troops to walk slowly towards the German lines. But when the bombardment began, the Germans simply moved underground and waited. Around 7.30am on 1 July 1916, whistles blew to signal the start of the attack. With the shelling over, the Germans left their bunkers and set up their positions. As the British walked towards the German lines, the machine guns started and the slaughter began. Although a few units managed to reach German trenches, they were driven back. By the end of the day, the British had suffered 60,000 casualties, of whom 20,000 were dead.

Years later, Alf wrote (picture 89) about his unexpected and emotional meeting with Ted in Flanders, just twenty-four hours before the Battle of the Somme:

> *That reminds me of our meeting in France. It was on the Somme, 24 hours before the greatest bombardment of the war. By some underground means, we were aware of each other's whereabouts. How excited we were. What a lot we had to tell – but how little we told. We just sat on the shell-torn wall and ate the chocolate Ted had brought. But the chocolate nearly choked me, and as for the enjoyment of our meeting it was like Tiny Tim's toast – it had no heart in it. No Man's Land with the knowledge of approaching calamity is no place for brothers to meet. We knew each one would be caught up in the horrors of attack and defeat.*

A postcard he sent home shows that Alf was at one point hospitalised, so he suffered some sort of injury, though there is nothing to suggest that it was serious (picture 90). When his sister Clara died in 1916, Alf wore a black cloth-covered button as a sign of mourning: although this was unofficial and strictly not approved of by the military, it was usually overlooked (picture 91).

When the war was over Alf returned to Cardiff, though he soon moved out to Langstone. In 1921 when he was running Priory Nurseries with his younger brother Herbert, Alf married 27-year-old Mabel Witts, the younger sister of Charles Witts who had married Alf's sister Fanny in 1916; so Alf had probably known her for some years. Mabel was a music teacher, and lived at 21 Riverside Terrace, Ely, close to the Palmer family home in Mill Road. In 1921, Alf and Mabel had a son, also called Alf, in 1927, but he died soon after he was born. In February 1929 Mabel died in childbirth in a Newport nursing home.

I should perhaps record here that a family member told me, with some conviction, that Alf and his brother Albert were employed on the building of the Empire State Building in New York City. However, construction took place in 1930-31, by which time the brothers were settled in Wales. With an open mind I did investigate further but found that no records of employees (mostly immigrants) who worked on the site exist. It is possible that there is a thread of accuracy in the story, because in the very early years of the century when the brothers *were* in the USA the skyscraper building-boom was in full flow. But having said all of that I have not found any record that suggests that they were in New York other than when they both briefly passed through in April 1913 having arrived by ship from England, and when Alf sailed from there to England in January 1916.

Alf remarried in 1932 to Gwen Saysell, who had two daughters from an earlier marriage, namely Joan born in December 1916, and Billie born in December 1921. Alf and Gwen had one daughter, Mary, who was born in 1934. Gwen died in 1948, Mary died unmarried in 2000, and Joan died in approximately 2008.

Politically, Alf was the most 'left-wing' of the brothers, most of whom had socialist leanings notwithstanding that, by and large, they were eventually financially comfortable and had seen considerable success in their various businesses. Alf was on familiar terms with senior Labour Party personalities, and he met and corresponded from time to time with

Prime Minister Harold Wilson and Speaker George Thomas. He was a keen supporter of trade unionism, having joined the Bricklayers' and Stone Masons' Union of America when he was in Vancouver (picture 92).

By the 1940s Alf was living at Cathonen, Langstone. One day in 1943 while out walking, Alf picked up a small, pointed piece of rock. It turned out to be a Bronze Age flint arrowhead, which he gave to the Newport Museum where it is now exhibited.

Through the 1960s and 1970s Alf was living at Bramley, Catsash Road, Langstone. In 1967 he announced to his somewhat surprised family that he was to marry again, to Vera Louise Keene, the daughter of a good friend of his younger brother Herbert. Vera had been viewed as a lifelong spinster, but she and Alf married and lived at 'Silverdale' in Magor Road, Langstone. A former resident of Langstone told me that Alf carried a great deal of weight in Catsash Road, with meetings to discuss local issues and problems being held in his house.

Alf died at his home in October 1975. Vera survived him by twenty-five years.

25

Home thoughts from the New World

*T*he following are extracts from Alf's diary of 1913, transcribed verbatim by his daughter Mary in 1970. Alf wrote short sharp entries on most days, but despite their brevity he was able to convey humour and sadness. Mary prefaced her transcription thus:

> *Alfred James Palmer, aged 21, with his brother left Cardiff in the early hours of April 12th 1913, in search of work in Canada. In his baggage, a small green diary – a parting gift from Auntie Ri – wishing him Health and Prosperity. Now copied from original black-lead entries nearly half a century later by his daughter.*

Mary's mathematics were slightly awry, as she transcribed the diary at Christmas 1970, 57 years after the events it describes. Alf's final entry on 31 December read: *'Hope the words of 1914 Diary will be more cheerful than those of 1913'*. I don't know whether or not he kept another diary: if he did I don't know what happened to it, but given the way that world events unfolded in 1914 it is unlikely that his hopes were realised.

Fri 11 Apr: Left Ely 11.15pm. Feeling sad leaving home. Good home and good family.

Sat 12 Apr: Went around Liverpool. Unfinished Cathedral. Feeling homesick. On board *Mauretania* for pm. Queer sensation at throat at sight of England vanishing.

Mon 14 Apr: Woke early. Had to run to lavatory. Sick. Didn't die there. Went back to bunk to die. Steward yelled '*Tell the Captain*'. Helpless. Chicken broth. Began to wish for end of journey.

Tue 15 Apr: Woke early. Sick again. No food. Struggled onto deck. Being anniversary of 'Titanic' widows on board throw over wreaths. Sea fairly rough.

Fri 18 Apr: Saw welcome land. Statue of Liberty. So weak could hardly carry bag. Very warm. Ellis Island. Ferry. On boat was stacked in for two hours. Feeling better

Thu 24 Apr: Arrived Calgary. Strolled around town. Found plenty of workmen out of work. Feeling downhearted.

Fri 25 Apr: Looking for work. All over city. Room and board Mrs Caffell 323 11ᵗʰ Avenue W. $6 a week.

Sat 26 Apr: 250 bricklayers walking about. Getting downhearted.

Mon 28 Apr: Looked for any sort of honest work but all full up. Begin to wish I was home. Very cold. Received letters from home.

Tue 29 Apr: Ground covered with snow. But started on Herald Block at 1pm. 67 cents per hour. 5 storeys up. Bitter cold but decent job (picture 93).

Wed 30 Apr: Twenty bricklayers stopped – overtaking carpenters. Spent afternoon looking for work. Feeling ill, miserable and disappointed. Give anything to see the beautiful hills and fields of South Wales.

Tue 6 May: *Accession of King George V, 1910]* Another day for the King. Couldn't find work anywhere.

Fri 9 May: Snow stopped after having fallen for 50 hours. Again out hunting for work. Getting desperate. In the evening had promise of work on the Herald Block on Monday morning. Feeling brighter.

Sat 10 May: Writing letters in the morning. Nice day. Baseball match in Victoria Park. Edmonton v Calgary. Excitable crowd.

Sun 11 May: Went to Chapel at 11. Evening service. Told to write to our mothers. After service went with Welsh chaps and had jolly good sing. Wrote to mother.

Mon 12 May: Started at The Herald. 8am. Stopped again at 10.30. Hoist broke down. Easy job. Accident – chap caught in hoist. Strolled around town in evening. Ice-cream on strength of getting job.

Tue 13 May: Getting used to swinging scaffold 9 storeys high. Another accident. Chap fell down. Cut head. Later went underneath to boilers. Good job. Told not to kill myself. Quite willing.

Wed 14 May: In the evening had letter from home saying about death of Grandfather. Went to bed with mixed feelings of sadness and thankfulness. Could not sleep, thinking of home and all who are there.

Tue 20 May: Worked all day on Herald. Warm. Plenty of fine dresses here – more like Paris.

Sat 24 May: *[NOTE: Interestingly, the day the author's father was born]* Got ready for day's shooting. Went down for letters but none there. Shot about 3 dozen gophers and some birds. Got back tired and hungry 7.15pm. McCartney *[McCarty]* killed at Tommy Burns Arena (picture 94).

Sun 25 May: Service early morning. Young Men's Own. Impressive

National Service in evening: Subject '*Our Imperial Citizenship*'. Rev Marshall. Reference made to boxing match. Fearless denunciation of Tommy Burns. National Anthem. Crowded congregation.

Mon 26 May: Read in paper of Tommy Burns' answer to Rev Marshall. Tommy Burns Arena burned down. Some people think he did it intentionally, thinking no more boxing. People think boxing will be stopped.

Sat 31 May: Another start looking for work. Got my money at 9 o-clock. 62 dollars 75 cents. 93 hours. Sent 25 dollars home.

Wed 4 Jun: Worked all day on CPR Hotel. Have to work harder than ever. Had a tiff with the Foreman about plumb-rule which was a little out. Fixed it, better in evening.

Thu 5 Jun: Stopped at CPR Hotel at 9am. Not sorry. Tramped about for half an hour and got a start on Albertan Block at 10.30am. Good job. 70 cents per hour. Told to take it cool which I did.

Sat 14 Jun: Gave notice, as we had intended going down East as my job would not last long and there was no other work about. Packed our trunks and took our leave for Medicine Hat.

Sun 15 Jun: Arrived Medicine Hat about 3am. Very cold and dark. Went out to Red Cliff in afternoon. Nothing doing. Very tired. Luggage not come. Took train to Moose Jaw. Most miserable Sunday ever spent.

Mon 16 Jun: Arrived Moose Jaw. Chinaman's lodging house: $33\frac{1}{2}$ cents. Roughest ever been in. Sleep after hiding our money, etc, expecting to be robbed every minute.

Tue 17 Jun: Chap has to be careful or else he would soon go under as we are now, but thank God we have our health and strength and each

129

other, and we are bound closer together by our misfortune.

Wed 18 Jun: Woke up tired and miserable. After having asked God's guidance through the day, went and found our luggage at station. Caught 11 train to Regina. Glad to get out of Moose Jaw. Wondering what Mother would think if she saw us there. Arrived 12.30. Room and board: King, 2041 Slinger Street.

Thu 19 Jun: Out at 8.30 looking for work. Union here very poor. Both disgusted at meeting here previous night. Consequently many scab jobs. Tempted to work scab. Regina town of Cyclone 30 Jun 1912. Hundreds of tons of debris lying about.

Fri 20 Jun: Surprising how happy we are although out of work.

Tue 24 Jun: Strolling around for work. Saw where man had been killed on Lyalls job. Fragments of clothing, boots, etc, about. Worked stopped. Cold and miserable. Went to Oklahoma Wild West Show. Very poor. One dollar.

Wed 25 Jun: Brickies delegate to speak at General Meeting when Leckie's job would be explained. Result was nothing arrived at. Consequently don't know what to do. Gave weeks' notice at King's.

Fri 27 Jun: Home early. Had sing-song and bed after keeping the house awake with our clutter.

Sat 28 Jun: Chased a snake 30' long.

Tue 8 Jul: Stopped in all day. Bought bottle of wild strawberries. Think will stop sickness. Got better.

Thu 10 Jul: Went out to gaol expecting to find work but were disappointed. Discouraged and tired we went back to lodgings.

Tue 15 Jul: Met Mr King. Told they wanted men to unload bricks. Started at 1pm. Hard work. Worked 'til 7. Hour's walk back to lodge. Very tired as it is the first work I've done for over a month.

Wed 16 Jul: Very tired at night: nearly fell down with stiffness. Asked for bed. Told to go to loft. Took blanket to hay loft. Had bundles of overalls stolen. Did not sleep for mosquitoes and mice.

Mon 21 Jul: Up early and off to work. CPR car holds 20,000 to 27,000 bricks. Capacity of some 100,000 lbs. Had hard blow with the bricks falling on me.

Tue 22 Jul: Saw the Printer from Glasgow 'beating it' down track from Med Hat to Winnipeg. Pitiful sight to see such fellows roughing it.

Wed 23 Jul: Good dip in bucket of very cold water. Beginning to enjoy camp life. Had a chat about Lloyd George.

Sun 27 Jul: Went to service at Baptist Church. Splendid sermon on '*The Comforter*'. Caught 10 o'clock train to Victoria Plains Very hungry, but no supper.

Mon 28 Jul: Had good breakfast and off to work at Grand Truck Depot.

Tue 29 Jul: Day at Grand Truck unloading truck of steel. 100,000 lbs. Very tired at night with hands blistering.

Thu 31 Jul: Steam plough in next field with 14 knives to it. Hard day's work by myself at CPR keeping two trolleys of bricks going. Handled 16,000 bricks.

Sun 3 Aug: In the evening went to Baptist Church. Heard address to boys on '*Burn Your Smoke*'. Good singing and crowded chapel.

Wed 6 Aug: Promise of a start through Mr MacGregor at Sherwoods store on Monday morning. Went to Lodge meeting at night. Forgot the password. Rush out at 9.45.

Sat 9 Aug: Started at Sherwoods 7 o'clock. 70 cents an hour, which is union wage. Hard slogging job.

Mon 11 Aug: Worked all day on Sherwoods. Still slogging. Job will soon be up. Has to be open October 1st. Had £5 sent from Father. Wrote letter and sent it back to him.

Thu 14 Aug: Awoke early at 2.30 by siren. Heavy thunder. Heaviest storm in history of place. Storm was on for over three hours. Sherwoods basement was flooded, so no work. Tools etc floating about. Flooded cellars etc all over city. Cars stopped, etc. Another terrible storm.

Sun 17 Aug: Service at Metropolitan. Sermon '*Cry of Humanity Today*'. Yet these Canadians do not preach Gospel. Saw Alb off to gaol.

Thu 21 Aug: Worked until 9 on Sherwoods. Got paid off 10.50. Went straight on to gaol. Nothing on for a week.

Mon 1 Sep: *[Labour Day]* Donned white trousers, white shirt and brown tie for Parade. Started off with band at 10.15 holding Bricklayers' banner. Float highly commended. Carpenters won shield. Enjoyable day.

Tue 9 Sep: Up and worked all day on gaol. Though very dusty. Firm had to issue goggles for us to wear. Eyes very sore through dust.

Wed 17 Sep: Worked all day on gaol. Men grumbling about food.

Thu 18 Sep: Did not work. Passed morning in bunk. Very cold and rough. Afternoon went out to shoot but came across threshing outfit and helped thresh. Men came from city drunk. Fight with cook, etc.

Sat 4 Oct: Started on West Wing of gaol. Caught train to Regina.

Sun 5 Oct: Went with Amos to Presbyterian. Good sermon on '*Saloons*'. Went to Presbyterian at night. Subject: '*How To Make A Good Wife*'. Train to Vic Plains.

Sun 12 Oct: Went to organ opening at Metropolitan Wesleyan. Organ cost $8,000. Went again at night. Splendid service. '*Hallelujah Chorus*' played. Vic Plains.

Wed 15 Oct: Alb goes to town sick. News of Welsh Colliery accident. 400 killed at Senghenydd.

Thu 16 Oct: Had heap of letters from home.

Wed 22 Oct: Started on St Chad's College. Went to City Hall. Lecture on Scotland and Wales.

Fri 24 Oct: Bricklayers' meeting at night. Old Age Pension voted for.

Sat 1 Nov: Went on lake with new boots. Had two hours. Were last to leave ice. Got on fairly well. Northern Lights.

Wed 5 Nov: Caught Imp Line to Moose Jaw where Navin Brothers are advertising for bricklayers. Got the job on the Armoury (picture 95). Rate same as Regina. Back to Regina. Prairie fire.

Thu 6 Nov: Train for Moose Jaw two hours late. Started on Armoury 1.30. Wrote to Alb. Went to Library. At 8 heard Dr Spencer at Baptist.

Sun 16 Nov: Caught train to Moose Jaw at 10.35. Arrived at 12.15. Just after two boys went through ice and drowned. Service at Zion Meth.

Sun 23 Nov: Attended Temperance Meeting afternoon. Splendid meeting. Hundreds turned away.

Tue 25 Nov: Attended convention of Temperance Workers. Prohibition proposals carried. Premier Scott attends with Attorney General. In sympathy with proposals. Splendid gathering of all shades of religion.

Mon 8 Dec: Took the shack on 2240 Argyle Street. Alb goes in on Wednesday. I stay 'til next Monday.

Thu 11 Dec: Nice cake from Em to Alb.

Mon 15 Dec: Went to Parliament Buildings to hear '*Banish The Bar*' bill introduced, but very disappointed.

Tue 16 Dec: Went to Buildings again, and still the Bill was not brought up. Heard it had been given up.

Thu 25 Dec: 15° below zero and the coldest day so far. Went to service at Knox. At 6pm went to banquet provided by Brotherhood of Met. Had a fine time. Thoughts mostly of home and those around the family table.

Wed 31 Dec: Thoughts of home and others. Went to Watchnight with Fred at Metropolitan and thus saw the Old Year out and the New Year in. Hope the words of 1914 Diary will be more cheerful than those of 1913. Goodbye.

65. Fanny and Charlie Witts, approx 1918.

66. Albert Palmer & Charlie Witts, and their bicycles.

67. Charlie Witts & Alfred Palmer in uniform, World War 1.

68. Nancy Witts.

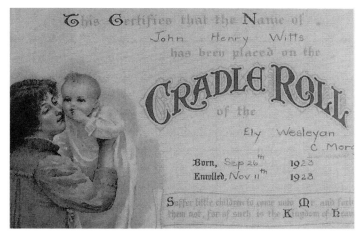

69. Cradle Roll certificate for John Henry Witts.

70. Pugh's grocery store, City Road, Cardiff.

71. Nellie Fox, approx 1900.

72. Jack & Tom Palmer, approx 1918.

"SANTA CLAUS" IN FLAMES.

EXCITEMENT AT A CARDIFF PARTY.

SET ON FIRE BY CANDLE ON CHRISTMAS TREE.

Just at the crucial moment when Santa Claus was disposing of his gifts to the children a burning accident, which might have had serious consequences, occurred at an Ely residence on New Year's Eve. Mr. E. Palmer, of Durston House, Mill-road, and his wife were giving a children's New Year party.

Everything went merrily until it came to the Christmas tree distribution. Mr. Palmer, in traditional Santa Claus attire, had entered the room to the sound of joyous shouts of the "kiddies," when in reaching for a toy his costume was ignited by one of the illuminating candles.

Before anyone present realised what had happened Mr. Palmer was enveloped in flames. The carpets had been taken up for the occasion, and so there was nothing handy with which to smother the flames. With great presence of mind Mr. Palmer's brothers stripped him of his fancy raiments. Not, however, before he had been severely burned about the face and arms.

A local nurse first treated the injuries, and Dr. Campbell, of Cowbridge-road, who happened to be passing in his motor at the time, was summoned and rendered further necessary attention.

Mr. Palmer was lying in bed when a *Western Mail* representative called upon him on Thursday night. His arms and face were swathed in bandages, but he was in cheerful spirits. He remarked that the consequences might have been more serious but for the timely help of his brothers.

73. Report of fire incident, Western Mail, 2 January 1914.

74. Alfred (seated) & Ted Palmer, World War 1.

75. Embroidered card sent by Ted from France, approx 1916.

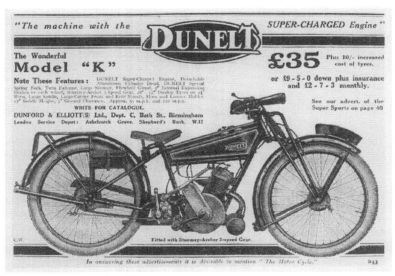

76. Dunelt motorcycle, 1926.

77. The Palmer brothers, some wearing Lodge regalia. L-r: Alfred, Herbert, Edwin, Walter, Albert & William.

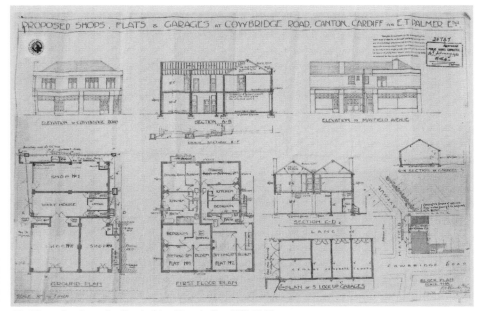

78. Plans for shops in Cowbridge Road, Cardiff, 1933.

79. Letterhead for ET Palmer and Sons, grocers.

80. Palmer's Stores, 514 Cowbridge Road, Cardiff.

81. Ted Palmer, President of Cardiff & District Grocers' Association.

82. Ted Palmer, President of the National Federation of Grocers' Associations.

83. The authors parents Tom & Cissie
Palmer, Porthcawl, late 1930s.

84. Nellie and Ted Palmer in the South of France, 1950s.

Mrs Palmer is 100

A CHAMPAGNE party in a flower-filled marquee was the way Mrs Nellie Palmer celebrated her 100th birthday.

Her family had been planning the special treat for weeks which included a congratulatory telegram from the Queen.

Mrs Palmer, of Victoria Park Road West, Cardiff, was born in Barnsley, Yorkshire. She came to Cardiff with her family when she was four. She married Mr Edward Thomas Palmer, who had a grocery business in Cowbridge Road West, and had three boys and one daughter.

She has 11 grandchildren and 20 great grandchildren.

There were 96 relatives and friends at the party organised for Mrs Palmer at the home of her daughter, Mrs Winnie Treseder in St Lythan's.

Mrs Palmer's two sons, Gordon and Tom, had also helped in organising the marquee on the lawn filled with pink and white flowers.

"She had a fantastic time and we've got it all on video," said Mr Gordon Palmer.

Mrs Palmer will probably enjoy watching her starring role on film for she likes watching television and reading romantic novels, poetry and history.

85. Report of Nellie Palmer's 100th birthday, South Wales Echo, 1 September 1987.

School dresses for 100th birthday

IF you see children wandering around the Albany Road area of Cardiff this week in unfamiliar costume, "don't worry — they're only getting into the swing of their school's centenary celebrations.

Throughout this week they'll be attending Albany Road Primary School in Victorian dress as the school embarks on a string of events to mark its one-hundredth birthday.

Hordes of parents, pupils and ex-pupils crammed the school premises last Friday to see Cardiff West MP Rhodri Morgan open the school's centenary festivities.

He stepped in to save the day after Viscount Tonypandy, who was to have conducted the opening, fell ill.

All 420 children at the school have contributed to the school's exhibition which is open to the public until Thursday.

It includes historic photographs and cuttings from the South Wales Echo over the years.

And there's a mock-up of an 1887 school room to give an idea of what it was like when the Albany Boys' School, as it was then known, opened with Mr Edmund Willmott as headmaster.

A few old faces could still remember the first headmaster and it was appropriate that Nellie Palmer, aged 100, of Victoria Park Road West, and assumed to be the oldest living ex-pupil, should cut the birthday cake.

Dressed for the occasion in Dickensian costume, headmaster Mr David Lloyd paid tribute to the hard work of staff and youngsters in making the exhibition a success.

He added: "We felt it would depict what has gone on over the 100 years. All the staff and children have been very enthusiastic and I am absolutely delighted with it."

The school's oldest former pupil, Mrs Nellie Palmer, 100, cuts the centenary cake with headmaster Mr David Lloyd.

86. Report of Nellie Palmer, aged 100, at school centenary celebration, South Wales Echo, 9 November 1987.

87. Alfred Palmer (third from left) in a captured German staff car, World War 1.

88. Alfred Palmer (far right), Northern France, approx 1916.

IT WAS TED WHO PROTECTED 'KITCHENERS LONG ARM TO THE DEEP SOUTH AND BROUGHT ME HOME TO WHERE MY TIME AND THE COUNTRY HONEY IN THE BLOOD AND FILTH OF FLANDERS.

THAT REMINDS ME OF OUR MEETING IN FRANCE IT WAS ON THE SOMME 24 HOURS BEFORE THE GREATEST BOMBARDMENT OF THE WAR. BY SOME UNDERGROUND MEANS WE WERE AWARE OF EACH OTHERS WHEREABOUTS. HOW EXCITED WE WERE. WHAT A LOT WE HAD TO TELL – BUT HOW LITTLE WE TOLD. WE JUST SAT ON THE SHELL TORN WALL AND ATE THE CHOCOLATE TED HAD BROUGHT. BUT THE CHOCOLATE NEARLY CHOKED ME, AND AS FOR THE ENJOYMENT OF OUR MEETING IT WAS LIKE TINY TIMS TOAST. IT HAD NO HEART IN IT. I WISHED WE HAD NOT MET.

WILL NOT UNDERSTAND. TED WILL. NO MANS LAND WITH THE KNOWLEDGE OF APPROACHING CALAMITY IS NO PLACE FOR BROTHERS TO MEET. WE KNEW EACH ONE WOULD BE CAUGHT UP IN THE HORRORS OF ATTACK AND DEFEAT.

89. Alfred Palmer's recollections of the Battle of the Somme in 1916, written in 1959.

90. Alfred Palmer (centre) in field hospital, World War 1.

91. Alfred Palmer, wearing black mourning button, 1916.

92. Alfred Palmer's union banner.

93. The Herald Building, Calgary.

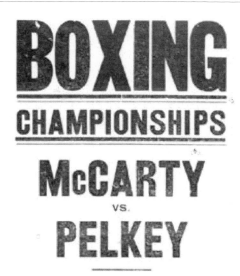

94. Boxing poster, May 1913.

95. State Armoury, Moose Jaw.

96. 15th Cardiff Boys Brigade. Corporal Walter Palmer is in front row, second drummer from left, probably about 1910.

97. Walter Palmer in uniform, World War 1.

98. Walter Palmer,
drummer World War 1.

99. Mabel Palmer.

100. Walter & Mabel Palmer.

101. Herbert Palmer.

102. Herbert & Walter Palmer, and a bear.

103. John Lush Palmer & Amelia Lucy Palmer.

104. Walter Palmer's son Leonard, and Emma Jane Palmer's son Ernest, World War 2.

105. John Beard, with portrait and subject, at Art Gallery of New South Wales, 2007.

106. Palmers Drive, Ely, Cardiff.

107. The author.

108. The Fox & Goose, Coombe Bissett.

26

The drummer boy

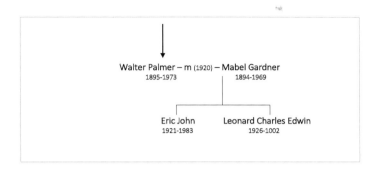

```
                          │
                          │
                          ▼
    Walter Palmer – m (1920) – Mabel Gardner
         1895-1973                  1894-1969
                          │
                   ┌──────┴──────┐
              Eric John      Leonard Charles Edwin
              1921-1983           1926-1002
```

alter Palmer was born in 1895. As a young lad Corporal Walter
Palmer was a drummer with the 15th Company of Cardiff Boys
Brigade (picture 96). Walter acquired horticultural skills working as a
teenager on the family nurseries in Ely, although the war brought a pause of
several years. During The Great War he again played a drum after joining
the Royal Army Medical Corps, though his main role was as a stretcher-
bearer with the Field Ambulance division of the Corps (pictures 97 and
98). Attached to an army Division, the Field Ambulance was a mobile
frontline medical unit (not a vehicle), with responsibility for the care of
casualties in the Division. In theory, the capacity of a Field Ambulance was
150 casualties, but in battle they would often be overwhelmed by numbers.
The Ambulance was responsible for establishing and operating a number
of points along the casualty evacuation chain, from the Bearer Relay Posts
which were up to 600 yards behind the Regimental Aid Posts, through the
Advanced Dressing Station to the Main Dressing Station. It also provided
a Walking Wounded Collecting Station, as well as various rest areas and

local sick rooms. In addition most large field ambulances had a drum and fife band, and this is undoubtedly where Walter's drumming skills were employed when Ambulance duties permitted.

After the war Walter (sometimes known as Wally) returned to the nurseries and lived again in Mill Road. He married Mabel Gardner (picture 99) in 1920 and they had two sons, Eric in 1921 followed by Leonard born on Christmas Eve 1926, by which year they had moved to Fairwater, Cardiff (picture 100).

In January 1939 Walter obtained planning permission to build nurseries, initially called Glebeland Nurseries, and a house, in Wenvoe on the main Cardiff-to-Barry road, and soon he started to run what in due course became Sunnydale Nurseries, the site of which is now a pub and hotel. He frequently won cups for his wonderful shows of flowers, especially dahlias, at horticultural shows across South Wales, and in due course a new trophy, the Sunnydale Cup, was introduced as a consequence of his successes. He also helped to cultivate the 'Bishop of Llandaff' dahlia referred to earlier.

Unfortunately, although he ran a thriving business, in the post-war years Walter was reluctant to modernise, to the frustration of his sons who wanted him to join the trend for garden centres, seen by most as the way forward. But Walter was finding it hard to move with the times. Instead, dedicated to the Methodist Church and being of a kindly nature, he gave much of his money to good causes and became somewhat behind the times in terms of business management, lacking the shrewd business acumen of his brothers. Like his brother Alf he was a close friend of George Thomas, perhaps closer than Alf. Thomas was a Methodist lay-preacher as well as a Cardiff MP, and would in due course become Speaker of the House of Commons, and he often visited Walter in Wenvoe. Through his connections with the family, but notably Walter, he preached regularly at Ely Methodist Church and once at Langstone Methodist Church.

Walter died in April 1973: for some while he had been living in a caravan at Wenvoe.

27

A kind heart

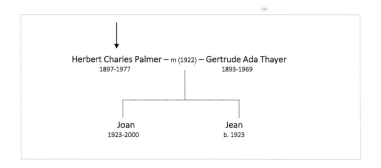

Herbert Charles Palmer — m (1922) — Gertrude Ada Thayer
1897-1977   1893-1969

Joan   Jean
1923-2000   b. 1923

John and Amelia's last child, Herbert Charles Palmer, was born in 1897. As a young child Herbert used to enjoy trips by train from Ely to Rumney to stay with his uncle Bill Shute (Amelia's brother) and Bill's wife Esther. But on one such visit Herbert nearly died when he fell into a sewer on Rumney Moors, but was saved by Ted and his friends who pulled him out. Herbert served for part of The Great War, probably in the Royal Field Artillery. Up until the war he had lived at 35 Cowbridge Road, although at one point during the 1920s, when he was suffering ill health, he went to live with Ted in Mill Road. To cheer him up, Ted gave him one of the earliest tins of Heinz Baked Beans seen in Wales.

Herbert (picture 101) moved out to Priory Nurseries, Langstone, where he worked with his brother Alf, and when visiting the family in Ely he would often travel via Canton, just a mile or two from Ely, to collect manure from stables for the nursery. Living there was a lady called Gertrude Ada Thayer, (known as Ada) who had never known her parents: her mother had died young, and her father had been killed in an accident while alighting from a cab. Herbert proposed to Ada and they married in 1922; the following year they had twins called Jean and Joan.

Some time later Herbert became acquainted with a severely disabled lady named Melita; she had never walked and despite being in her forties she prayed every day that she would one day be able to walk. Her only form of mobility was a wheelchair, which in reality was more like a carriage. Herbert used to send the nursery's van to take her to and from the doctor's surgery. In due course, Herbert and his sister-in-law Nellie decided to take Melita to Switzerland to enjoy the clean climate, and while there she continued her nightly prayer regime. Then one morning, after hearing noises in her room at night, she found she could walk, an event regarded by Melita and all those she knew as a miracle.

Later in life Herbert lived in a house called '*Oakleigh*' in Langstone, which he bought from the builder. Very shortly after the sale the builder was killed in a car accident, and Herbert's kind-heartedness again came to the fore as he allowed the builder's widow to stay in the house. In the 1960s he moved to Porthcawl, and at one point he also bought a hotel in Ogmore-by-Sea, on the Glamorgan coast, called '*Brigadoon*' (picture 102). Herbert died in Porthcawl in 1977. Tragically, his daughter Jean's husband died after only thirteen months of marriage.

28

The end of an era

*A*melia Lucy Palmer outlived her husband John by 29 years, and died in Langstone in January 1949 aged 90. An interesting insight into her character can be found in her Will, which she executed a year before she died. Before leaving her residual estate to her sons, she made just one specific bequest, namely to Kamal Athon Chunchie, a Methodist minister and the founder of 'The Coloured Men's Institute' in Victoria Docks, in the Canning Town district of London. Born in Ceylon (now Sri Lanka) to Muslim parents, Chunchie had converted and worked for the Wesleyan Methodist Missionary Society among the Asian, Chinese, African and Caribbean sailor community in Canning Town, where he spoke out against racism and the plight of the dispossessed, invoking the Christian ideals of equality and brotherhood to combat racism while unmasking the hypocrisy of Christian England and its attitudes to race, which he saw as incompatible with Britain's Christian values. In 1923 he founded the Docklands' first black Wesleyan Methodist church. An accomplished speaker, Chunchie (who played cricket for Essex) toured the country preaching at Wesleyan

Methodist churches, and it seems probable that Amelia heard him speak in either Langstone or Cardiff and that she followed and supported his missionary work. It is revealing that she chose this man to be the only non-related beneficiary in her will.

Amelia's parents Albert and Clara, and her grandfather Thomas Crowden, are buried in the cemetery at Llandaff Cathedral; so are other family members including Amelia's three-year-old sister Maria Jane, who died in 1868, and her 20-year-old brother Albert who died in 1897.

John and Amelia's sons mostly lived to a good age. The exceptions of course were the babies Ernest and Ivor: my father, Tom, was given the middle name Ivor in memory of the latter, who would have been his uncle. The infants Ivor and Ernest are buried in Cathays Cemetery, Cardiff, where they lie together.

John and Amelia are buried at the Parish Church, Langstone. They too are together (picture 103).

Aftermath

I must now delegate the task of continuing the story. In order to complete individual accounts I have made brief mention of some events close to the end of the twentieth century; but there has been no firm end-point for my contribution. If there is to be a sequel, it should begin around the start of the Second World War, when there will undoubtedly be stories to uncover and tell.

I will however leave the reader with a few updates which might prove helpful should anybody take up the challenge. These are by no means comprehensive, and for reasons of brevity I have picked out a few illustrations and undoubtedly overlooked much of what the recent and present Palmer generations have been doing. Like their ancestors, recent generations have been hardworking and family-orientated people, and I mean no disrespect by omitting the achievements of those I do not mention.

At least four of John Lush Palmer's grandchildren served in the Second World War, namely Ted Palmer's sons Gordon and Jack, Emma Jane's son Ernest, and Walter's son Len. In fact Ernie and Len met by chance in

North Africa, rather as Ted and Alf had done in France in 1916 (picture 104). I am sure that other family members also served in the war.

Emma Jane's grandson, John Beard, became a world-renowned artist who won many prestigious awards, had studios in several countries, and exhibited in the world's top museums and galleries including many across Australia, in New York, Madrid and Lisbon, and in London at the Tate, Whitechapel Gallery, Royal Academy, Science Museum and National Portrait Gallery (picture 105).

Ted Palmer's grocery and greengrocery store in Cowbridge Road Cardiff was for many years the hub of the local community, and was run by Ted's sons Tom, Jack and Gordon until it was closed in the late 1970s and the property sold to Lloyds Bank. Ted's granddaughter Cheryl Treseder exhibited regularly and won awards at the Chelsea Flower Show, and his grandson Richard was librarian and archivist to the Archbishop of Canterbury at Lambeth Palace.

The nursery business founded by John Lush Palmer in Ely was managed successively by his son William, and then by William's son Ron who in 1965 moved the business to Pembrokeshire in West Wales; there Ron's son Gareth took over the reins until the business closed in 2007. A housing estate was built on the site of the nursery in Ely, and one of the roads is named 'Palmers Drive' (picture 106).

The close connection with Ely Methodist Church that began when John Lush Palmer moved to Cardiff continued, and John's sons Ted, William and Walter were church trustees well into the 1960s. The family connection still continues as I write this.

As for me, I was a civil servant working for the Lord Chancellor for most of my adult life, although perhaps more interestingly – and certainly more enjoyably – I played guitar in rock bands for many years until researching for and writing this book took over my spare time (picture 107).

The Fox and Goose at Coombe Bissett continues to supply the thirsty and hard-working folk of Coombe Bissett, and no doubt many who pass through the village (picture 108).

I leave you with some important lessons I have learned, and which I pass on especially to younger readers. If you want to know about current and recent generations, ask the people who know before it is too late. If you keep old photographs, whether on paper or stored digitally, make a note of who is shown in them, the date and the occasion. Remember that future generations may be interested in *your* story, so keep diaries and share your experiences.

And finally learn about, understand and respect your heritage, because it has probably made you the person you are today.

– Appendix A –

How we got to me

Edmund Palmer (1530 – 1598) m Emma
↓
Richard Palmer (c 1560 – 1641) m Parmeller
↓
Edward Palmer (c 1590 – c 1672) m Christabel Parsons
↓
Edward Palmer (1628 – 1681) m Margaret Whitmarsh
↓
Edward Palmer (1662 – 1727) m Sarah Benwell
↓
John Palmer (1695 – 1786) m Mary Barber
↓
John Palmer (1736 – 1788) m Sarah Barber
↓
John Palmer (1771 – 1802) m Mary Harwood
↓
Charles Palmer (1797 – 1854) m Mary Orchard
↓
John Palmer (1826 – 1913) m Hannah Lush
↓
John Lush Palmer (1858 – 1920) m Amelia Shute
↓
Ted Palmer (1889 – 1971) m Nellie Fox
↓
Tom Palmer (1913 – 2007) m Vesta ('Cissie') Matthews
↓
Ray Palmer (b 1946) m Judith ('Judi') Palmer

– Appendix B –

Sketch map of Wiltshire, showing towns and villages mentioned in the story

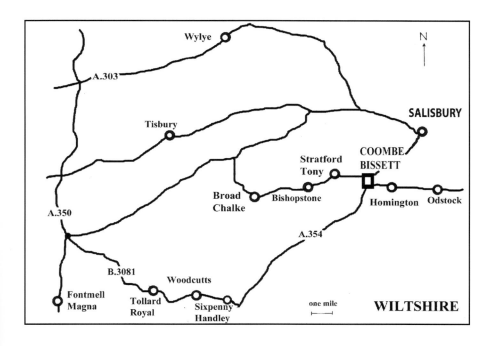

– Appendix C –

Acknowledgement of assistance, sources
and references

I must make special mention of three family members who have contributed significantly to this project. First, my cousin Richard Palmer who drew a family tree that first set me off on this journey, for his help and encouragement throughout the writing process, and not least for his impressive ability to unearth ancient records and decipher mediaeval script.

Next, my second cousin Stephen Palmer (whom I did not know previously) who responded to a 'cold call' enquiry with a superb store of photographs and documents, and who I'm pleased to say still lives in Langstone.

Finally my wife Judi who, despite having minimal interest in my family history has endured the massive piles of papers around the house and was patient through my frequent and lengthy spells in front of my computer.

Many photographs and recollections have been submitted by members and friends of the family, including some early contributions from my aunt, Winnie Treseder, who sadly passed away before the book was complete.

I am grateful for the assistance given to me by officials at Glamorgan Archives Cardiff, Wiltshire and Swindon Records Office Chippenham, The Library and Archives Canada, Dakota Sunset Museum, Gettysburg SD, USA, The New York State Archives, The New York City Municipal Archives, The Avery Architectural and Fine Arts Library, New York City, and The Library and Museum of Freemasonry.

From time to time contributors to Facebook groups, most notably 'Remember Ely', 'Cardiff Now and Then', 'Remember Old Cardiff' and

'Glamorgan Family History Society', have helped and offered research suggestions, for which I am grateful.

The following are reproduced by kind permission of Wiltshire and Swindon Records Office:

Will of Emma Palmer, 1598

Will of Edmund Palmer, 1598

Will of Edward Palmer, 1773

Will of Edward Palmer, 1727

Will of John Palmer, 1802

Inventory of assets, John Palmer, (extract) 1802

The following are published courtesy of Glamorgan Archives:

Plans for 12 houses, Mill Road, Ely (RDC/S/2/1908/83)

Plans for additional bathroom 23 Coveny Street (BC/S/1/15301)

Plans for 3 shops & 2 flats, Cowbridge Road (BC/S/1/28747)

Photograph of Sidney Ernest James Read, (DHGL/11/14)

Information about streets and residents was obtained from:

Butcher's Cardiff Street Directory 1880-81, 1882-83

Post Office Directory 1871

Cardiff Commercial Directory 1882-83

Kelly's Directory 1891

Cardiff Directory 1897, 189, 1894, 1914

Minneapolis City Directory 1902, 1903, 1904, 1915

www.historicaldirectories.org

The history of the name 'Palmer' is quoted by kind permission of *The Internet Surname Database*, www.surnamedb.com 1980 – 2015, with statistical data quoted from Forebears.co.uk.

Extracts from '*A Thumbnail History of Coombe Bissett*' are included by kind permission of Wiltshire and Swindon History Centre http://history. wiltshire.gov.uk/community/getcom.php?id=70

The story of Charles Meaden the wheelwright is from Jane Howells and Ruth Nerwman, eds, '*William Small's cherished memories and associations*' (Wiltshire Record Society vol 64, 2011), p. 72

The quotation from *Birdsong* by Sebastian Faulks, published by Random House, is included by kind and personal permission of the author

Information about weaponry used by Ernest James Beard in WWI is included by kind permission of Brian Eves, author of http://www. hackneygunners.co.uk

Details of Albert John Palmer's service with the Canadian forces is included by kind permission of The Library and Archives Canada, and of his time in Forest City by kind permission of Dakota Sunset Museum, Gettysburg SD, USA

The photograph of Charles Tanfield Vachell is reproduced by kind permission of Cardiff Council Library Service

I have accessed two websites in order to verify and correct some of my own research regarding the Green family. They are the websites of Howard Green and Chris Roughan http://familytreemaker.genealogy. com/users/g/r/e/Howard-W-Green/ and http://chrisroughan.webs. com/racesandstringers.htm

Reports of trial of Thomas Green from: Howell, Cobbett & Jardine (1783) *A Complete Collection of State Trials and Proceedings for High Treason and Other*

Crimes and Misdemeanours from the Earliest Period to the Year 1783', Volume 344

The two extracts from the *South Wales Echo* re Nellie Palmer are reproduced courtesy of Media Wales Ltd

The title of Chapter 24 *'Staunch To The End Against Odds Uncounted'* is from *For The Fallen* by Lawrence Binyon

The copy of the annotated score of *The Waggoner* is reproduced by kind permission of The Vaughan Williams Charitable Trust

The photograph of Moose Jaw Armoury reproduced by kind permission of The Army Cadet League of Canada, www.armycadethistory.com

The photograph of John Beard is reproduced by kind and personal permission of the photographer Kate Geraghty, and by permission of Fairfax Syndication, New South Wales

The photograph of the author appears by kind permission of Julia Wainwright and of Mitchell Palmer Ltd.

General information on various subjects was sourced as follows:

Cardiff and its industries: http://www.cardiffians.co.uk, http://dicmortimer.com/2011/06/20/vanished-cardiff/, and www.localhistories.org/Cardiff.html

Aberdare: http://www.cvhs.org.uk

Primitive Methodism: http://www.engleseabrook-museum.org.uk/history.asp

The decline of agriculture in Wiltshire: Ensor, RCK (1936) *England, 1870-1914, The Oxford History of England,* Clarendon Press

The First World War : http://www.bbc.co.uk/history/worldwars/wwone/battle_somme.shtml, and http://www.ramc-ww1.com/index.html

Post-war riots in Cardiff: http://www.walesonline.co.uk/news/local-news/riots-streets-cardiff-poverty-hits-2092740

Warings Brickyard: http://www.rumneyhistory.org.uk/

The work of a gas stoker: http://www.johnhearfield.com/Gas/Gas_strike.htm and http://188.65.112.140/~daftscou/steve/Twenties2.htm

The Methodist Historic Roll: www.familyhistorypartnership.co.uk

The Passive Resistance Movement: Cardiff Times 22 April 1905
Births, marriages and deaths: www.gov.co.uk, www.ancsestry.co.uk and www.findmypast.co.uk

Probate records: www.gov.uk/wills-probate-inheritance.